THE SOUL OF SURFING

Fred Hemmings

Thunder's Mouth Press
New York

Published by
Thunder's Mouth Press
841 Broadway, Fourth Floor
New York, NY 10003

Originally published by Sports Enterprises, Hawaii
First Thunder's Mouth Press Edition 1999

Hemmings, Fred. 1944-
[Soul of surfing is Hawaiian]
The soul of surfing / by Fred Hemmings.
p. cm.
Originally published: the soul of surfing is Hawaiian. Maunawili, Hawaii : Sports Enterprises, c1997.
ISBN 1-56025-205-7
1. Surfing—Hawaii. I Title.
GV840.S8H448 1999
797.3'2—dc21 98-55933
CIP

Manufactured in the United States of America

Rell Sunn...
your soul is surfing

Dedicated with love...

Fred, Suzy and the Hemmings Family

Introduction

by Paul Holmes

Philosophers have long pondered the nature of the human soul and argued over its corporeal seat. For those whose thoughts are directed mostly to the pursuit of wave riding, however, there is universal agreement that the soul of surfing is to be found in Hawaii, and its essence suffused with Polynesian culture. This book by Fred Hemmings—Hawaiian wave rider and canoe paddler, businessman, politician and tireless promoter of the sport of professional surfing—owes its title to these axioms of surfing, but also gives the nod to a deeper meaning for those who have confronted the raw power of crashing ocean waves. Unlike most sporting activities, surfing generates in its participants an almost religious awe for the beauty and energy of waves, and of the sea that gives birth to these mysterious forces of nature. Many surfers speak of riding waves as a Zen experience, as an artform, as a lifestyle—not in the weekend magazine sense of trendy habitat and designer accessories, but as a form of vocation with a deep spiritual significance. It is a perspective that stands in stark contrast to the stereotype of surfers as bronzed, blond airheads with minds flushed clean of thought by the constant pummeling of death-defying wipeouts.

Of course not all wave riders share the transcendental view of surfing, and few insiders would have predicted its acknowledgment by one as down-to-earth and pragmatic as Fred Hemmings. But as this book will show, surfing is a passion for individuals of diverse backgrounds, opinions, and attitudes: moguls and dropouts, liberals and conservatives, rich and poor, weekend warriors and full-time professionals—all equal once they paddle into the lineup of towering swells. Out in the ocean, everyone faces surfing's thrills and terrors essentially alone. Perhaps for this reason, surfing seems to breed strong individualists. It is a sport—or art, or daily spiritual ritual—that unites mavericks of many shades and stripes.

That Hawaii is the mecca of world surfing is an undisputed fact. Since modern surfing began in the late 1950s, with the introduction of lightweight foam and fiberglass boards making surf travel adventures logistically feasible, Hawaii has been a place of pilgrimage for surfers. No surfers worth their salt are considered fully experienced until they've ridden waves in Hawaii. Even at the highest echelon of today's professional surfing, international competitors cannot earn the respect of their peers until they've gone head-to-head against the massive waves of Oahu's North Shore in winter. Here, along a dozen miles of unique beaches and reefs, the world's biggest, most powerful, and most perfectly formed waves are to be found. Here, surfing has established the high altar of an open sky cathedral whose naves and chapels are the entire Hawaiian Island chain. The spiritual home, the seat of surfing's soul, however, remains in Waikiki.

While nobody can be absolutely sure that Hawaii is the birthplace of surfing, these islands are certainly where wave riding was developed and refined. Surfing was completely unknown to western civilization until Captain Cook and his crew witnessed canoe surfing in Tahiti in 1777. The following year, in Hawaii, the *Endeavour's* crew recorded their first sight of surfboard riding. In those days standing upright on long wooden boards was reserved for the ruling class; surfing was literally the sport of Hawaiian kings and queens. Ironically, after missionary zeal discouraged many aspects of the indigenous Polynesian culture, surfing almost died out in Hawaii by the end of the nineteenth century, and it took interest from European and American adventurers, including the writer, Jack London, to help revitalize the sport in the early 1900s.

Another wandering journalist, Alexander Hume Ford, surfing and living by his wits in the tropical ambiance of turn-of-the-century Waikiki, formed the Outrigger Canoe and Surfboard Club in 1908. The intent, according to its fund-raising charter, was to make Waikiki "always the Home of the Surfer . . . to spread abroad the attractions of Hawaii, the only islands in the world where men and boys ride upright upon the crests of the waves." London had already done his part by writing about surfing for the *Woman's Home Companion* magazine, and later he used that article as the basis for a chapter in his popular novel *The Cruise of the Snark*.

In 1911, the Hawaiian and part-Hawaiian surfers of Waikiki formed their own club, Hui Nalu—club of the waves—with its HQ in the basement of the Moana Hotel, one of the few large structures on Waikiki's still pristine, palm-fringed shores. Members from both these clubs were the first generation of Waikiki's beach boys—legendary swimmers, surfers, canoe paddlers, and fishermen in the Hawaiian tradition—whose fun-loving, laid-back lifestyle would be emulated by surfers everywhere as word of the sport spread around the globe.

Among the founding members of Hui Nalu was a local boy, still only 16 years old, who, in 1912, become an Olympic swimming champion. In the course of a long and spectacular subsequent career, his international travels, competitions and exhibitions brought surfing to far corners of the earth. So, during the first half of the twentieth century, Waikiki local and full-blooded Hawaiian, Duke Paoa Kahanamoku, became surfing's first international ambassador and the universally recognized "father of surfing." Duke was a superb athlete, skilled board rider and living embodiment of the ancient Hawaiian spirit. He defined the soul of surfing for successive generations of wave riders and will likely do so forever.

Fred Hemmings grew up in Waikiki when the beach boy era was still in its prime, before exponential development and tourism inexorably changed the erstwhile paradise. Like countless others over the years, Hemmings studied the surfing style of the beach boys, listened to their stories, and was inspired by their prowess in the ocean. As a teenager he even joined their ranks, working on the beach.

As his own surfing skills developed, Hemmings became a successful competitor. In 1958, at age twelve, he surfed for the first time in the Makaha International Championships, a forerunner of today's well-orchestrated international professional events. In 1963 he won its junior division. As surfing became more organized during the 1960s, Hemmings was enlisted as a member of the Duke Kahanamoku promotional surfing team, part of an emerging surf industry producing boards, clothing, and accessories for the burgeoning lifestyle-sport. In 1968 he won surfing's amateur World Contest in Puerto Rico.

It was a bittersweet victory. The still embryonic sport of surfing was going through a sea change. The social disruption of the hippie era was rippling through surfing's ranks, and the call to "turn on, tune in, and drop out" struck a sympathetic chord among many who had already adopted a lifestyle out of synch with societal norms. Simultaneously, the sport of surfing was undergoing a profound metamorphosis in equipment, with once-standard 9- to 10-foot surfboards weighing 20 to 30 pounds being replaced almost overnight by much shorter, lighter models that performed quite differently. Not only was Hemmings firmly in the conservative, "establishment" camp of surfing's divided social order; the board he rode in Puerto Rico, and hence his style of surfing, was also considered less than cutting edge by the new era's cognoscenti. In terms of the kudos usually afforded world champions, Hemmings' victory was in many respects overshadowed by history. Only in retrospect is it now acknowledged that the official results were correct. By following the rules—catching the five biggest waves and riding them the longest distance—Hemmings' classic competitive approach had rightfully won the day.

Fred Hemmings' greatest legacy in surfing, however, will not be his World Title. During the 1970s and 1980s, Hemmings became a highly successful promoter, bringing together a season of top flight professional contests in Hawaii that were televised nationally as part of the prestigious ABC Wide World of Sports, setting the stage for surfing to become legitimately professional. In the mid 1970s, he formed International Professional Surfing (IPS), that coordinated the first international circuit of pro events, with a system of accumulated ratings points to determine an overall World Champion each year. In those early, often tumultuous years, his hands-on experience as a contestant, entrepreneurial talent, and conservative (small c) mind set made him a formidable leader and earned him the begrudgingly respectful moniker "Dead Ahead Fred" among the first generation of pro surfers. While Hemmings' role as a promoter and administrator was often controversial, and although he ceded power in 1983 in what was essentially a coup d'état by a group of his own pro tour players, Hemmings' vision and often thankless hard work today results in a multilevel world circuit with more than $5 million in annual prize money and events held in more than a dozen countries. Hemmings' contribution, enabling hundreds of surfers to make a living from their chosen lifestyle, remains invaluable.

Hemmings' persuasive personality and diplomatic skills were put to a very different purpose from 1984 to 1990, when he was elected to Hawaii's State House of Representatives where he went on to become minority leader, and eventually ran, albeit unsuccessfully, for Governor on the Republican ticket. During his term in office, Hemmings introduced legislation to protect Hawaii's surfing reefs by extending State Park boundaries offshore beyond the tide line. It was a concept, he says, consistent with traditional Hawaiian views (and law), that did not separate the resources of land and sea, and considered shore and reef as part of a natural continuum. The bill failed to pass, but it illustrates clearly the soul of surfing he tried to bring to the legislature. Today he laughs about the dichotomy of being a surfer in politics: "When I was campaigning I was constantly labeled as a surfer," he says. "People would say 'what does a surfer know about politics and business?' Now, of course, when politics is finally out of my system and I'm back to being just a surfer again, I'm labeled as a politician and businessman."

As a partner in a successful restaurant and a state representative for the National Football League, Fred Hemmings is still very much the Hawaiian soul surfer. With this book of recollections and reflections, he records a unique time and place whose echoes still reverberate throughout the surfing world. He also offers fascinating insight into the sport's Hawaiian roots for anyone who has ever marveled at surfing and those who ride, as Jack London described surfers at Waikiki almost 100 years ago, "not buried and crushed and buffeted by those mighty monsters, but standing above them all, calm and superb, poised on the giddy summit."

Waikiki, the Cradle of Surfing

I love "talking story." Surfers sometimes take as much pleasure from sitting around talking about surfing as they do actually surfing. This is especially true of older surfers, who can stretch the truth and not have anyone around to dispute it. In fact, you should have seen the 33-foot wave I rode backwards at Makaha in 1961, when I was out alone with surfing legend Rabbit Kekai, who said, "dats nothin'," as he recalled that he caught a 34-foot wave.

Duke and I were talking story. I asked him how he achieved his legendary 1-mile ride across the bay of Waikiki from Castles surf to the beach at the Royal Hawaiian Hotel. He answered that no one could get a ride like that anymore. I was taken aback at first. It sounded almost like Duke was bragging. He went on and explained, "Freddie, the waves no longer break all the way through to shore. When they built the Ala Wai canal in 1923, they cut off the streams that emptied into the bay of Waikiki. The bottom of the ocean changed, the waves have changed, too…forever." Duke's eyes sparkled with memories of the surf he grew up in. Duke was not bragging, he was lamenting the changes that had altered the waves of Waikiki.

How wonderful that the Hawaiians were the people to harness the surf as a source of pleasure. For thousands of years cultures living and prospering on the coastlines of the world's great oceans viewed waves as an adversary of nature.

Where many saw difficulty, the Hawaiians saw fun. From the seductive waves of Hawai'i was born the sport we now call surfing. The waves of Kalehuawehe, Makaha and Paumalu are, to this day, the source of legends.

We get a glimpse of Waikiki, "the cradle of modern surfing," from the reminiscence of G.W. Bates, who wrote in 1854:

> *Within a mile of the crater's [Diamond Head] base is the old village of Waikiki. It stands in the center of a handsome coconut grove...there were no busy artisans wielding their implements of labor; no civilized vehicles bearing their loads of commerce, or any living occupant. Beneath the cool shade of some evergreens, or in a thatched house reposed several canoes. Everything was so quiet as though it were the only village on earth; and the tenants, its only denizens.*
>
> *A few natives were enjoying a promiscuous bath in a crystal clear stream that came directly from the mountains; some were steering their frail canoes seaward; others clad in Nature's robes were wading out on the reefs in search of fish.*

From this idyllic setting, modern surfing came to the eyes of the Western world.

The feat of riding waves was viewed by Western culture with astonishment. From Captain Cook's expedition came this observation of surfing:

> *...the boldness and address with which we saw them [the Hawaiians] perform these difficult and dangerous maneuvers was altogether astonishing and scarce to be credited.*

Captain Cook's voyage and the subsequent migration of Americans, Europeans and Asians thrust Hawai'i into a world exploding with change.

Hawaiian surfing ambassadors took the sport to foreign shores early in the twentieth century. Waikiki surfer George Freeth, who is credited with introducing surfing to California, is believed to be the "brown Mercury" eternalized by Jack London's prose:

> *Where the moment before was the wide desolation and invincible roar is now a man, erect, full statured, not struggling frantically in that wild movement, not buried and crushed and buffeted by those mighty monsters, but standing above them all calm and superb, poised on the giddy summit, his feet buried in the churning foam, the salt smoke rising to his knees, and the rest of him in the free air flashing in the sunlight, and he is flying through the air, flying forward, flying fast as the surge upon which the stands. He is a Mercury—a brown mercury. His heels are winged, and in them is the swiftness of the sea.*

The patriarch of modern surfing, Duke Kahanamoku, had a life-long affair with the sea. His mistress, the waves, kept a smile on his face and gave him the passion to share his love with all those he encountered. He took surfing with him wherever he traveled. In 1915 Duke taught the Australians to surf at their Clearwater Beach. Duke popularized surfing on the East Coast, and those he taught to surf on the waves of Waikiki were soon venturing out onto the waves of their homelands. From the hearts of the Hawaiians, surfing was spread with aloha.

On the banks of Apuakehau stream in the middle of Waikiki was founded the first modern-day clubs devoted to surfing and Hawaiian canoe racing—the Outrigger Canoe Club and the Hui Nalu.

The Makaha International Surfing Championships, inaugurated in 1954, became the world's first truly international event. Much of the criteria and methods of producing modern surf competitions originated at the famous Makaha Championships. Peruvians, Australians, Californians and surfers from around the world eventually found their way to Makaha.

Surfing *ali'i* like Keaulana, Kekai, Aikau and Rell Sunn are held in high esteem in the wave world.

Hawaiian surfing is fertile with culture and ancient folklore. Contemporary sports—football, basketball, tennis and golf—have a history of roughly 100 years. The legends of surfing were part of ancient Hawai'i's mythology when Captain Cook sailed to Hawai'i over 200 years ago. Kalehuawehe, known now as Castles surf, and Paumalu, now called Sunset Beach, are the mystical surfing sites chanted in the ancient oral history of these islands we call Hawai'i.

Professional surfing gained stature and prominence in the wide world of sports with the development of pro events on the North Shore. The Smirnoff, Duke, Pipeline Masters and World Cup events are the pioneer competitions of modern-day pro surfing. These events, through television coverage, popularized the sport of surfing to the masses. The worldwide pro surfing circuit was conceived and inaugurated in Hawai'i. The ultimate test for the surfing elite are the formidable waves of Hawai'i.

Even now, the boundaries of wave riding are being pushed by the innovations of Hawai'i's surfers. The incredible exploits of "tow ins" into the jaws of death-defying waves is a quantum leap into another realm of surfing. Hawaiian surfers are preserving a heritage born on the alluring waves of Hawai'i, He'e Nalu, surfing.

The genesis of surfing is traced to the ingenuity of the ancient Hawaiians. The cradle of modern surfing is Waikiki. The celebrated legends of surfing journey through time on the waves of Hawai'i.

Surfing is Hawai'i's gift to the world.

Waikiki, Surfing's Fertile Crescent

In ancient times, Waikiki was an idyllic village. The name Waikiki roughly translates to "spouting waters." Three major streams—Pi'ianio, Apuakehau and

Kukenauahi—emptied cool, fresh water from the valleys of the Koʻolau mountains into the Pacific Ocean. Freshwater springs gurgled with the best drinking water in the world. Nearby taro patches were the source of food. The ocean supplied a cornucopia of fish. The gentle and alluring waves of Waikiki made it the playground of kings.

By the start of the twentieth century, the vestiges of old Hawaiʻi were disappearing. Mosquitoes, brought by a whaling ship to Hawaiʻi, were marauders that irritated all who visited Waikiki. In 1923, the Ala Wai canal was built to drain the ponds, with the intent of eliminating the mosquitoes and "building up" the land. The fabled streams expired, freshwater springs were buried, and the Waikiki of ancient Hawaiʻi all but disappeared. At the time, what was done may have seemed prudent. How I wish it had been otherwise.

By 1950, Waikiki was a neighborhood community and the epicenter of a burgeoning tourist industry. The Royal Hawaiian Hotel was built in 1927 in a fabled grove of palm trees called Helu Moa. The Moana hotel, built at the turn of the century, was situated on the Diamond Head side of Apuakehau stream. Waikiki was still home to various prominent local families. By mid-century, many of the beachboys and surfers lived in an area called "the jungle," at the Diamond Head end of Waikiki. It consisted of a series of cottages. On the beach fronting Canoes surf, next to the Moana hotel, were grand old homes that had been turned into commercial sites.

Kalakaua Avenue is named after the "Merrie Monarch," King David Kalakaua, and is the main street through Waikiki. When going to the beach in those days, you could park on Kalakaua Avenue within a very short distance of where you wanted to go. Lei sellers still had huts fronting the lush grounds of the Royal Hawaiian Hotel. Across from the Outrigger Canoe Club was a parking lot under a huge banyan tree that, as legend has it, was planted by Princess Kaiʻulani. The parking lot is now the International Market Place.

The best part of Waikiki was the people. Waikiki was home to many great surfers.

This was the Waikiki I first remembered.

Now, over 35,000 hotel rooms choke Waikiki.

Cradle of Surfing

Many old-timers and downtown business types stored their boards in wooden lockers in Waikiki at the original Outrigger Canoe Club site. This was in the mid-1950's. I used to sit under the *hau* tree, where the Hui Nalu gang hung out, and watch the parade of surfers go in and out.

One well-built Hawaiian gentleman whom I frequently saw walking out to the ocean with his board wore what I thought at the time were very strange swim trunks. He had on tank shorts. All the surfers starting with Duke Kahanamoku wore classic beach surfing shorts. This dignified Hawaiian looked rather odd in his black tank shorts. I found out that he was Reverend Akaka, the pastor of Kawaiahaʻo Church. I don't think Reverend Akaka will remember this, but we talked after I got to know him. One of my religious pursuits at the time was surfing. Reverend Akaka, a wise man, understood the ways of youth. I will always remember that he once referred to Waikiki as the "cradle of modern surfing." As the years go by, that has more and more meaning.

Surfing was a dying pastime as Hawaiʻi struggled into the twentieth century. The cultural changes thrust on the native Hawaiians were profound. Surfing was getting lost. On the sands of Waikiki the founding father of modern-day surfing, Duke Kahanamoku, grew up near what is now the Hawaiian Village hotel. A hundred years ago, it was a quiet coastline on the way to Waikiki beach. Piʻianaio stream emptied into the Pacific not far from Duke's family home. Duke and his brothers were children of the sea and soon all became proficient in swimming, surfing and outrigger canoe paddling. On Waikiki Beach, Hawaiians and their youthful friends from Honolulu town preserved the surfing sport as part of their lifestyles. Surfing was joyfully shared by these men and women with visitors from around the world who came to the sleepy little resort area called Waikiki.

Being a small kid at the time, I did not realize that the men and women whose shadows I grew up in were the great founding legends of modern surfing. Duke, his brothers, Dad Center, John D. Kaupiko, Joe Akana and Lorrin Thurston are among the legendary names that should always be honored in surfers' memories.

Reverend Akaka said it so well those many years ago, "Waikiki is the cradle of surfing."

The Surf Sites of Waikiki

Imagination is one of children's greatest toys. Most kids have imaginary friends and make imaginary forts or doll houses to play with. I bet many surfers, when they were small kids, spent hours imagining the ultimate surf paradise. The great thing about being a kid growing up in a playground called Waikiki was that I lived in a surfing paradise. I used to draw maps of the surf sites in Waikiki, putting in detail every coral head, sand bar and current.

At the Diamond Head side of the bay a bunch of friends frequented a break called **Tonggs,** named after a family that lived on the beach called, in ancient times, Kaluahole. Tonggs surf even has a little peak called the **Winch,** which is actually one of the only remnants of a square rigger that sunk there near the turn of the century. The Tonggs regulars included, at one time or another, surf legend Paul Strauch, current Hawai'i judge Eric Romanchek, Robby Estes, Rusty Starr, my cousin Tomi Winkler, Donny Mailer and, of course, the Tongg brothers—Ronny and Michael.

Rice Bowl is a "kick *okole*" left slide that is next down the line. Rice Bowl, during a good south swell is, in my opinion, the hottest tube in town. It is a hard spot to photograph—hence, the lack of notoriety. I am sure the regulars are happy surfing in obscurity—"more waves for me, brah."

Next, on a sand bar outside the reef is a break called **Old Mans.** Old Mans fronts a natural channel known in ancient times as Kapua. I am an Old Mans regular, despite my youth(self-delusion). The reef on the other side of the channel obstructs any good surfing, except on southwest swells with a little size. That rare break is called **No Place.** Don't sit on Kaimana Beach and wait for it to happen.

On huge summer swells, the legendary waves of **Kalehuawehe** break out in deep water. This mystical surf's modern name is **Castles.** We want to keep it "mystical."

On the edge of the reef peeling into Waikiki is **Publics**—on the inside is a body boarders' break called **The Wall.** Outside on a larger swell is **Cunhas** break.

Rice Bowl, neat wave, neighborhood break, no hassles. In 1983 my pal Warren Bolster snapped this photo as I dropped in on my Blue Max II. I liked the original Blue Max (1966), so I had a second version made over 20 years later. Check out the style on the bottom turn—looks like the Makaha Bowl shot on the cover of this book. What do they say about old dogs?

Queens is a neat little right slide that breaks off a sand bar reef. During my small-kid times you could ride waves early in the mornings with just a few body surfers. One morning on dawn patrol I was riding a wave at Queens with a body surfer. I guess I crowded Mr. Kalama too much. I fell from my board as he grabbed my tail while riding behind me. This was Noah Kalama, Ilima's famous dad and grandfather of Jaws daredevil surfer, David Kalama. We respected our elders. My reply was, "Sorry, Mr. Kalama, I won't get in your way again." He smiled. We had fun the rest of the morning. Queens has spawned many great surfers, including Allan Gomes and Joey Cabell from my generation.

I think you can safely say that people over 45 years old who surf in Hawai'i probably spent the early days of their surfing lives at **Canoes**. It was just so convenient. Canoes surf is a gentle wave that laps into the very epicenter of

I have been canoe surfing Old Mans since 1964, when this photo was taken. Surfers get out of your way when you are in a canoe. My aim is pretty good.

Waikiki. It is also famous for Canoe surfing—hence, the name. On the beach fronting Canoes surf is Waikiki's first major hotel, the dowager queen of Waikiki hotels, the Moana, built in 1901. Surfing's first clubs were founded on the shore, and certainly Canoes surf was the home break of modern surfing's founding fathers. When I first ventured out to what seemed the big waves of Canoes as an 8-year-old, there was a handful of regulars—my friends Wayne Miyata, Maurice Ikeda, Nappy Napoleon, the Achoy brothers, along with many of the beachboys—who shared the waves of Canoes.

Both Queens and Canoes have "baby" surfs that are inside of the regular break. As a young boy, I was admonished not to venture out past "baby" surf to the big 3-foot waves of Canoes.

Outside the bay of Waikiki, on the reef that runs all the way to Ala Moana, is a series of breaks starting with **Populars** and **Paradise.**

I can close my eyes and envision with great joy long sessions of riding 6- to 8-foot summer swells at **Number Threes,** with nobody out but a few friends. If there is one surfing site on the south side that is much unheralded, it would be Number Threes. The long right slide is *no ka oi,* "the best." In the early sixties, Number Threes was home break to many top athletes from the Outrigger Canoe Club. The "studs" were Ronnie Sorrel, Petie Balding and the late, great

Tommy Haine. These guys were also all-American volleyball players. Joey Cabell was a regular. The next generation of surfers included my brother Butchie, Gilly Halpern, Paul Maclaughlin, Tim Guard and a few others. I was low on the pecking order in those days.

Number Fours is next down the line (I always wondered what happened to Number Ones and Twos). It doesn't line up as well, as the swells wall up and collapse all at once on the reef.

Across the man-made Kaiser channel is a snappy break aptly named **Kaisers**. Kaisers is a hot little right slide breaking on a coral shelf on the edge of the channel. The industrialist who developed the channel and the Hawaiian Village hotel was Henry J. Kaiser. He was not a surfer, but his name stuck.

Rock pile is next. Like Number Fours, it goes no place fast. I am sure that there are Rock Pile regulars who will emphatically disagree with me. I hope they enjoy the Rock Pile surf. When I was chasing waves in the neighborhood, we did not have to frequent the break.

We call the first swell of summer, which usually hits in early May, the Mother's Day swell. This photo of Number Threes was snapped by Peter French on May 8, 1968. I was riding my first short board, 8'0", sounds like a semi-tanker, but alongside my customary 9'8" board it was short...er.

Donald Takayama, 1959, puts his best side forward in this "lost" photo. He claims his mother took his trunks away—sure, Donald.

I used to pack my board on my shoulder and walk from my home base on the beach at Waikiki to the hot spot, **Ala Moana.** Carrying my 30-pound board over the mile walk from the Outrigger to Ala Moana was hard. I was a motivated kid. The local hero at Ala Moana was "Birds Nest," a surfer who lived in the Kalia neighborhood near the break. He owned Ala Moana. His real name was Donald Takayama. The regulars included Bla Pahinui, Conrad Canha, Boogie Kalama, Gilbert Soyu, Peter Moon, John Kruse, Buzzy Knuebuhl and an entourage of colorful guys, many of whom ended up in the entertainment business. I can remember coming in after long surf sessions and sitting around while these guys held jam sessions and drank Primo beer. Ala Moana is really a man-made break, created when they dredged the entrance to the Ala Wai yacht harbor. It is a hot left with a bowl.

A south swell snapped over a very shallow shelf to form a dangerous right slide called **Garbage Hole.** It was just across the channel from Ala Moana. No one surfed it much. I loved the place. The goofy footers ruled Ala Moana, and I would often paddle across to Garbage Hole and surf alone. I learned, when needed, how to keep my body on the surface during a wipeout. I got rolled across the reef often, but somehow a 2-second tube was worth it. Garbage Hole no longer exists. It was buried by a man-made development called Magic Island. With a bit of smart planning, we could have had Magic Island *and* saved Garbage Hole. I'll save politics for later.

As a local boy growing up in Hawai'i in the mid-fifties and sixties, these Waikiki waves were my home. No crowds—I knew everyone who surfed the various breaks. Though from so many different backgrounds, we had in common a love for the ocean and riding the waves. We also respected our elders and heritage. What a blessing it was to surf in Waikiki then.

The Outrigger Canoe Club

My earliest recollections of surfing come from the shores of Waikiki at the Outrigger Canoe Club. The Outrigger was the first truly modern day surf club. It was founded in 1908 on the banks of Apuakehau stream. The rustic setting was on the beach between what is now the Royal Hawaiian and the Moana Hotel. The first club house was a grass shack. The club was dedicated to surfing, outrigger canoe surfing, canoe racing and social intercourse (I'll leave that one alone). Soon after the founding of the Outrigger in 1911, the Hui Nalu was started. These two clubs have produced some of Hawaii's most notable ocean athletes.

Hui Nalu boys gather in the grass shack near the Outrigger Canoe Club on Waikiki Beach, 1911. Wish it was still there. Check out the "short" board.

The Outrigger Canoe Club is where I spent the days of my youth from about 1953 till the club moved to its new site at Diamond Head in 1964. Those years were magical. At the old Outrigger, there were about 150 vertical wood lockers, where every imaginable type of surfboard was stored.

If you think some of the recent surfboard designs are original, think again. I can vividly recall a wide variety of surfboards in the lockers, including a swallow tail, a concave, various balsa designs, wooden removable fins pounded into a wooden box, even hollows and boards so old they were varnished. Some of the old-timers thought the new invention—fiberglass—was "waste time," meaning humbug.

In 1959, the first foam boards started showing up in Hawai'i. On the spacious beach, koa outrigger canoes were stored, just as they had been for 1,000 years. A new koa canoe is very difficult to come by in modern Hawai'i. If you can find the rare native koa tree, it would cost over $50,000 to make a canoe. Some of the canoes at the old Outrigger were close to 100 years old. Koa canoes were cherished and played a very prominent role in the daily lives of pre-contact Hawaiians.

By the time I was 10 years old, I was a regular at "right slide" Canoes. Most of the old-timers rode their big long boards and slid left, angling for the beach at the front of the Royal Hawaiian Hotel. All the hot guys were at right slide. For awhile, the bull of right slide was Jama Kekai, Rabbit's strong and tough brother.

The old-timers at left slide Canoes were intense. In my small-kid times I would not dare get in their way. They would run me over. I learned respect the old-fashioned way.

12

Coming Down

Small-kid time is also when I learned the etiquette of surfing. Now, 40 years later, it seems chivalry and surfing etiquette have disappeared.

When I first ventured out to Canoes surf, I lived in mortal fear of getting in the way of the old-timers.

I would sit inside, near the edge of the break. The old-timers would catch the bigger waves outside, turn their boards, and remain frozen in a stance as they rode across the face of the wave. They stood like car hood ornaments, poised on their boards. They would yell, "coming down," if they suspected one of the kids inside wanted to take off in front of them. I never did translate "coming down" exactly, but I knew what it meant. Back then, "coming down" meant "don't you take off in front of me, small kid, or I run your sorry little *okole* over with my big old balsa board." Yes—that's exactly what "coming down" meant.

First Break

When I was a youngster on Waikiki Beach, if you asked, "how big are the waves?" the answer could be..."First Break." You would know exactly what the surf was like.

During most of the summer, Waikiki waves would be 2 to 3 feet. As reported in Tom Blake's book back in 1935, some surfers still thought waves were a product of earthquakes. Others said moon phases made the waves come up. We now know that the summer surf in Hawai'i comes out of the southern hemisphere—a long way. That is why the waves in Waikiki never get as big as on the North Shore.

The unpredictable swells of my youth had very defined names to indicate size. Rarely would a surfer say, "Surf's up, it is 3 to 5 feet at Canoes." What you would hear was, "It's blow hole surf," which meant Canoes was breaking through the "blow hole." That translated to mean the surf was a little better than the normal 1 to 2 feet. First Break meant big waves in the vicinity of 6 feet at Canoes surf, breaking outside the regular lineup. Often, first break waves would back off and re-form in the normal lineup.

First Break was reserved for the "big guys." "Zero break" was a rarity—that is when Canoes was pretty well closed out and the big wave riders of the day would head out to Publics and Castles. Even Castles had different code names that are curiously sometimes heard today. *"Papa Nui,"* or big board, was the term Duke used for big Castles surf.

When the waves were 10 to 12 feet, the Castles lineup was called "Blue Birds" or "Steamer Lanes." Remember, old surfers tell incredible stories. The name "Steamer Lanes" came about because, when the waves were up, surfers would have to sit out in the ocean so far that they were in the "Steamer Lanes" of the big ocean liners. The older surfers get, the bigger the waves seem to get, as they think back to when they were in their prime.

Hui Nalu

Between the Outrigger and the Moana on the beach was a *hau* tree. Part of the tree is still on the beach. This is where the Hui Nalu gang hung out. Though an old club like the Outrigger, they did not have a clubhouse. At the Hui Nalu *hau* tree I learned how to take a midday nap—a very valuable skill. Hui Nalu's famous racing canoe, the *Lio Keo Keo,* or White Horse, was kept on the beach. Prince Jonah Kuhio, Hawaiian royalty, was a member of Hui Nalu early in the century. The Hui Nalu had a swim team, many of whose members represented the United States in numerous Olympics. Duke was a member of both Hui Nalu and the Outrigger, as some surfers were. Hui Nalu was considered the Hawaiian Club, and the Outrigger was considered the *haole* (Caucasian) club—which really did not make any difference to the fun-loving and competitive ocean athletes of both clubs. The friendly rivalry continues to this day. John D. Kaupiko was the celebrated leader and coach of Hui Nalu when I was young.

The unbeatable Hui Nalu team of 1912—Stroke John Kaupiko, No. 2 Harold Lishman, No. 3 Bob Kaawa, No. 4 Lono McCallum, No. 5 Captain Kaniau Evans, Steersman Duke Kahanamoku. The Hui Nalu athletes help preserve the sports traditions of their thousand-year-old culture.

Kala Kukea

Kala Kukea was what Hui Nalu canoe club is all about. The Kukea family had one leg firmly planted in modern Hawai'i and the other in ancient Hawai'i. Joe Kukea, the patriarch, married California surf star Ethel Harrison. Their sons Kala and Kahale carried their Hawaiian heritage on in a subtle manner. My friend Kala went to Kamehameha School for Boys and then went on to West Point. I raced canoes and surfed against him when we were young. After graduating from West Point, he served the cause of freedom in Vietnam. He was a hero. Kala was in the audience at West Point for General MacArthur's famous speech, "Duty, Honor, Country." Kala did his duty and honored his country and Hawai'i.

In 1976 I joined the Hui Nalu canoe club to paddle with them. Kala was the coach. We had several winning seasons together. Those were special years for me. Here was a guy who represented everything great about Hawai'i. He was, first and foremost, Hawaiian. Like his ancestors, he did not find a need to wear a shirt—and did so only when he had to. He did not need clothes to distinguish himself. He swam like a fish, surfed, and was one of Hawai'i's premier canoe paddlers and steersmen for over 30 years. He gave so much to the youth by teaching and coaching. Early in 1996, at 52 years of age, Kala died, part of Hawai'i died, part of everyone who loved Kala died. The heart of the Hawaiian culture beat in Kala's chest.

Waikiki Surf Club

There were numerous canoe clubs throughout Hawai'i—The Waikiki Surf Club, founded in 1948, was a powerhouse in canoe racing and surfing. The members of this club created the famous Makaha Contest in 1954 and started the prestigious Diamond Head paddleboard race. For many years, Waikiki Surf Club had a legendary canoe racing team. Dutchy Kino, Joe Gilman, Jeff Chee, Ants Guerrero, Randy Chun, Michael Tongg and the famous Blue Makua, Sr. and his son, Blue Makua. The late Blue Makua, Sr. was a hero of mine, as I watched him steer canoes when I was a young boy. Blue "felt" the temper of the ocean and steered an outrigger canoe with instincts inherited from generations gone by. The Waikiki Surf Club gang all hung out near the Kuhio area.

The Outrigger Canoe Club, Hui Nalu and Waikiki Surf Club shared Waikiki Beach in the days of my youth. These clubs and their members played a critical role in the evolution of modern surfing. There are no longer canoe and surf clubs on Waikiki Beach.

The Beachboys

If Waikiki and surfing had a "romance" era, it would have to be from about 1930 till 1960. This is when the famous Waikiki Beachboys were in charge of fun at Waikiki. The beachboys included Panama Dave, Steamboat, Turkey, Kaulakaua, Harry Robello, Sally Hale, Chick Daniels (conveniently, his pants fell down when he did the hula at the rowdy beachboy parties), Squirrely, Dingo, Richard Kao and Black Out—just to name a few. Actually, their business was teaching tourists how to surf and taking them for canoe rides. Many of the world's rich and famous came to Hawai'i, stayed at the Royal Hawaiian Hotel, and let their hair down with the beachboys.

The great appeal of these fun-loving guys was that they didn't care who you were or how much money you had. They would party almost every night after closing the beach service. I suspected many of the beachboys felt a very strong compulsion to try and put a smile on young ladies' faces. I had a friend who called the compulsion *"kokua the sisters." Kokua* means to help. I don't think the term *"Kokua the Sisters"* was intended to be literally translated. The beachboys were not bound to the "missionary" morals. These beachboys are now part of the folklore of Waikiki. They wrote the book on fun.

You may detect a mournful yearning on my part to turn back history to the time of my youth in Waikiki. It would be great to have the conveniences of modern technology combined with the space and freedom of a bygone era. The world today is too crowded, people need businesses, condos, hotels, cars and all the trappings of modern times that cramp our world. Are we going to blindly continue down the road of overpopulation? With visionary planning and incentives, we could create a steady, sustainable state economy and start to build down population. We will be damned if we don't.

Wave slashing, internationally acclaimed surfers like Michael Ho were weaned on the waves of Waikiki.

Waikiki was magic in the mind of
a young surfer growing up in Hawai'i.
Oh, Waikiki, how I dream of those carefree days
of my youth, now just cherished memories.

Duke
Duke Paoa Kahanamoku
Surfing Nobility

Entire books have been written about Duke Kahanamoku's lifelong adventures. Duke's achievements as a gold medal swimmer in several Olympics, in canoe racing, in Hollywood, as a goodwill ambassador, as the patriarch of surfing and the embodiment of aloha have all been well documented. However, I would like to tell you a few human interest stories about the fun I shared with Duke Kahanamoku.

This is a special photo. I asked Duke to sign this regal portrait, which was featured on the cover of Honolulu Magazine *in 1967. Duke wrote, in part, "to Fred, my favorite sufer." It was a subconscious slip, I think. We laughed.*

19

Moemoe – *"To sleep" in Hawaiian*

Duke could *moemoe* anywhere. I think it is a special gift God gave some Hawaiians. We once caught Chubby Mitchell sleeping, leaning against a palm tree. Anyway, I would always sit next to Duke at business luncheons and events. I would order a big meal and Duke would order a big meal, forgetting that he no longer had the ravenous appetite of a young surfer. I would help him finish his meal. Duke had a pair of high-tech sunglasses. Curiously, his sunglasses were like the ones in style now. They wrapped around the side of his head, and no one could look in from the side and see his eyes. At fancy meals and meetings, while all the business types were talking, Duke would put on his sunglasses and go to sleep. I remembered thinking...here is a man who has his priorities right.

Malibu Beach Babe

I have to explain that at the time we were on the Duke Surf Team, promoter Kimo McVay was on a roll with the Duke's night club in Waikiki. His main stage feature was a young Hawaiian entertainer named Don Ho. The Don Ho show was like a party every night, except customers had to pay. So, Don Ho was invited to debut at the Coconut Grove, the famous showroom at the Beverly Wilshire Hotel. Duke and his surf team—Paul, Butch and me—accompanied him. What a trip.

Kimo had arranged a promotional surf "safari" to Malibu. We traveled with Duke in a Rolls Royce. Arriving at Malibu, Duke said, "Go surf, boys, I'm going to sleep in the car." The waves were about 3 feet. It was a treat for me because I had never surfed the famed waves of Malibu before. By the way, I quickly figured out that it is easy to be a great surfer at Malibu for obvious reasons. After awhile, a crowd gathered on the beach. Was there trouble? What was happening? I paddled in, threw my board down and rushed up to the crowd. At first I thought, "Oh, no, I hope it is not a fight." There, dancing around on the beach was a totally naked, attractive young lady. Poor thing appeared to have ingested too many mind-altering chemicals. She was putting on quite a show. Jackie Baxter, a Malibu local, looked at Paul, Butch and me and let us know what gracious hosts they were at Malibu, providing great waves and entertainment on the beach, too. I am sure Butch wanted to join in on the dancing. Soon the police were running down the beach. Behind them, scurrying along as fast as he could, was Duke. The police officers wrapped the maiden in a blanket and hauled her off. Duke came up to us and asked, "what happened, boys?" We told him and he said, "Aw, shucks...next time, wake me up." Duke lived to be an old man but he always had a young man's heart.

The Duke Team went to surf at Malibu in style. Paul Strauch, Butch Van Artsdalen and I were the amigos on this trip. Duke would remember his Hollywood days and recount some amazing surfing and night surfing stories from the thirties.

Aloha Sneakers

The Duke Surf Team was scheduled to be at the Huntington Beach contest in 1965. We stayed at the Huntington Beach Sheraton, just down the road from the pier. Arrangements were made for us to visit the Randy Rubber Company, producer of sneakers. Part of the California surfing uniform in the sixties was a neat T-shirt, jeans, white athletic socks and "top siders," which was one of the popular brands of sneakers. The Hawaiians usually wore aloha shirts rather than T-shirts. The Duke Surf Team was under contract to Kahala Sportswear. We all had classic Hawaiian print shirts that Kimo McVay made us wear at public appearances. The gracious owner of the rubber (for footwear) company escorted Duke, Paul, Butch, Kimo and me on a tour through his factory. He explained that, through an adhesive process, they could stick almost any fabric to canvas to make various shoes in 12 minutes from start to finish. I looked at him and asked, "Could you make a pair of shoes in 12 minutes out of my aloha shirt?" He answered, "Yes." Duke was clever and quick. Before anyone else could say anything, Duke looked at me and said, "Freddie, take your shirt off and give it to him." I dutifully obeyed, and soon out of the machine appeared the first aloha print sneakers. They were kind of kooky but sold like hot cakes. Kimo McVay was elated. Butch, Paul and I eventually rued the day. Kimo McVay was like a den mother on these trips and used to literally tell us what to wear at various appearances. Kimo would coordinate our attire—one day Butch would wear his blue print aloha shirt and matching shoes, Paul's color would be yellow and mine would be red. The next day we would rotate colors. It was all too "cutesy," but, of course, the guy who was writing the checks, Kimo McVay, thought it was a PR dream come true…the Duke Surf Team color-coordinated in their matching aloha shirts and sneakers. That's Kimo.

We thought we looked like the three stooges and often received comments alluding to the same. On one occasion we were being given a VIP tour of Disneyland with Duke. Some smart-alec teenager spotted Butch and commented loudly to his buddies while pointing at Butch: "Hey, look, there goes Mickey Mouse now." Well, old Butch wanted to rip the kid's eyes out. Duke led the loud round of laughter at Butch's expense. After the initial anger subsided, even Butch started to laugh. P.S. I would give much to have a few pair of those original shoes now. Maybe there is some hot entrepreneur who will reproduce the aloha sneakers.

Last Wave

Duke loved the ocean. He was 76 and, after an illness that left him frail, he asked me to take him surfing. "Are you sure, Duke?" I asked him. He wanted to go surfing and instructed me to get out the huge, 13-foot board that was given to him for his 75th birthday. The enormous board was more a showpiece than a surfboard. I asked myself why is he wanting me to get out this board? I could barely carry it. Duke emerged from the locker room with a plastic seat cushion and a paddle. I put the board in the water. He sat on the cushion and paddled the boat-size board out to the edge of Old Mans surf. He caught a few waves sitting regally on his board, as the gentle waves carried him toward shore as they had done for over 70 years. He paddled back to the beach with a smile on his face. That probably was the last time he surfed.

What can I say about Duke? Why, so many years after his death, is he held in such high esteem? In the twentieth century, Hawai'i has seen many prominent industrial, political and civic leaders come and go. Yet, this surfer—Duke Kahanamoku—reigns supreme in the hearts of the people of Hawai'i.

Duke Kahanamoku was a man of virtue.

He was humble. Though he had many occasions to speak of himself and his achievements, he did not.

Duke was dignified. He always dressed and carried himself with dignity.

Duke was patient. On more than one occasion a well-meaning fan would come up and introduce himself and say something like, "Remember me, Duke? I met you in Atlanta in 1933 when I was 6 years old." Duke would smile and say, "Oh, how nice to see you again."

Duke was wise. Though lacking an extensive formal education, Duke had an intuitive sense about life.

Most of all, Duke was content. He had a sense of confidence that contributed to his dignified ways.

Duke Kahanamoku is surfing's greatest legend.

Thank you, Duke...

The Duke Classic — *It's legendary, too*

The Duke Kahanamoku Surfing Classic was inaugurated in 1965. Actually, it was the brainchild of promoter Kimo McVay, an event to honor Duke. I was employed by Kimo as his administrative assistant, in addition to being on the Duke Surf Team. I helped Kimo format the event. It was determined to make the contest a small, prestigious competition designed for television coverage. At the time the Makaha contest reigned supreme, with coverage on *ABC's Wide World of Sports*. We did not want to compete with the Makaha contest. It was decided to stage the event at Paumalu (Sunset Beach), which at first seemed to be a logistical challenge. That is how we ended up running the first few con-

The first Duke Classic contestants included Felipe Pomar of Peru, Mike Doyle—California, Paul Strauch surfing for Borneo—nah, Hawai'i, Corky Carroll—California (doesn't he look like the Joker in Batman?*), Fred from Portugal and the young man who won the first Duke Classic, Jeff Hakman, also known as Mr. Sunset. By the way, read Jeff's book titled, you guessed it,* Mr. Sunset.

tests from the porch of Val Valentine's house, directly in front of the peak of the Paumalu break. Kimo wisely hired Fred Van Dyke to be the contest director. Fred did a superb job of coming up with a list of 24 of the top surfers in the world to compete in the first Duke Classic. The concept of the Duke Classic was to have the very best of the best competing in a prestigious event. It was an honor just to be invited. The stage was set for the initial event to be held on the day the surf was best between December 13-17, 1965.

I have taken the liberty of ad-libbing titles to the list of the 24 pioneer contestants:

Robert "*Endless Summer*" August

Joey "speed surfer" Cabell

Corky "*California*" Carroll – *I always felt Corky epitomized the California surfer*

Rich "quiet but effective" Chew

Bobby Cloutier

Peter "I hate contests except the ones I am in" Cole – *he'll understand*

Mickey "Da Cat" Dora

George Downing

Mike "he man" Doyle – *This guy was an all-around surfer*

Jackie "young gun" Eberle

Skip "smooth" Frye

Jeff "the kid" Hakman

Fred Hemmings

Kimo "easy rider" Hollinger – *real laid-back*

Mike "slick" Hynson – *he looked like a movie actor*

Kealoha "Aloha" Kaio – *sweet guy*

Rusty "all star" Miller – *he was hot*

Mickey "let's party" Munoz

Greg "Da Bull" Noll

John "I am the greatest" Peck – *he exhibited substantial self-confidence*

Felipe "wild bull of Punta Rocas" Pomar – *earned the name winning the world title*

Paul "the gentleman surfer" Strauch

Butch "Mr. Pipeline" Van Artsdalen

Dewey "the little man on wheels" Weber

Kimo McVay had the Dodge Trophy Company of California design an Oscar-style trophy for each of the 24 competitors. The trophy is now one of the most prestigious artifacts of surfing. Pre-contest favorites included Paul Strauch, Mike Doyle, Joey Cabell and Rusty Miller. A press reception was hosted at the Moana Surfrider Hotel. The surfers had never been treated so well. The Duke Classic was further legitimizing the sport. The famous network surf event producer, Larry Lindberg, covered the Duke Classic for CBS. The competition was to be aired on the *CBS Sports Spectacular* in April of 1966.

The event was held on December 15, 1965. It was a mild day at Sunset, 8-foot-plus surf. Duke stood on the beach and watched. Seventeen-year-old Jeff Hakman surprised the surfing world with a victory. Jeff was still surfing in the junior division at Makaha and not considered a contender. The *Honolulu Star-Bulletin,* in reporting the results, noted that judges Wally Froiseth and Buzzy Trent both attested to Hakman's decisive victory. Second place went to Paul Strauch, third—to Felipe Pomar, fourth—Jackie Eberle, tied for fifth—Mike Doyle and Bobby Cloutier, seventh—Corky Carroll and eighth—Kimo Hollinger.

An awards ceremony was held at the Waikiki Shell. The Duke Classic, in its first year, immediately became a prestigious event befitting its namesake, Duke Kahanamoku. The event concentrated the level of competition and provided the foundation for surfing's growth as a professional sport. The Duke Kahanamoku Surfing Classic is a legendary event in surfing history.

In 1956 I was 10 years old, when this hot curl photo was taken. Surfers love photos of themselves, some sort of ego thing. That is probably why I still have this photo 40-plus years later.

Our family still considers the ocean a playground. My daughter, Meaghan, rode her first wave when she was a little over a year old.

Small-Kid Times

Family

I was the third of six children. My mother's family came to Hawai'i from Portugal in 1883 to work on a sugar plantation. My father came in 1922 from New York. My mother was a very devout Catholic, which did have an influence on me. Dad took up surfing and canoe paddling.

My older sister, Cynthia, led our family's surfing careers with success at the Makaha contest in the fifties. My brothers are Mark (Butchie) and Aka—both great watermen. They competed at Makaha and have won Moloka'i-to-O'ahu canoe races. You might remember that my brother Aka rode an incredible wave at Avalanche surf outside Haleiwa...in a canoe. Cynthia, Maria and Heidi are my surfing sisters. They, too, paddled and successfully competed in surfing events. Our playground was Waikiki Beach.

I grew up in a home of modest means (heck, we were poor). Dad sometimes worked two jobs to make ends meet. Mom bought some of our clothes from thrift shops. In 1951, I, along with three of my siblings, had polio. We were lucky, because the disease had no long-term effects. I had a rather sickly childhood, which I believe is what led to a life in the ocean.

All the children in the family went to Catholic schools when young and then we transferred to one of the finest schools in the nation, Punahou. It was expensive. We obtained financial aid scholarships. As a fifth grader in what was perceived to be a rich kid's school, I learned how crazy racial prejudice is. Being a somewhat loquacious young boy of part-Portuguese ancestry (it means I talked a lot), I was sometimes "da Portagee" at Punahou. I caught the express bus home after school and was the only kid to get off the Punahou bus in Kaimuki. Sometimes a few tough, local kids hanging around the bus stop would immediately hassle me as the f…. Punahou *haole* (Caucasian). I was not shy about responding. This occasionally led to a "beef" (fight) behind the Kaimuki theater. I learned to abhor people who promote class or racial strife.

At Punahou I played football. Coach Charley Ane taught me a lesson for life, how to win and how to lose. Losing is difficult. I also learned how to train hard, take my lumps, and not to give up. Winning and "giving lumps" is easier than losing and "taking lumps," and more fun, too. This had an effect on my surfing. By the way, we won the league football championships my senior year. I played with an incredible human being named Charley Wedemeyer. He was stricken with, and was supposed to die of, Lou Gehrig's disease years ago. Charley is alive because of his spiritual strength and a loving wife and family. He is one of my heroes in life.

I was 12 years old in the 1958 Makaha contest. My slightly (diplomacy) older sister Cynthia (right), third place and our family friend Kehau Kea (left), fourth place, were finalists in the women's division.

The best excuse I ever had for leaving church to go surfing before Mass was over . . .

My mom was on the Pope's all-star team. The entire family had to go to Catholic Mass on Sundays. Cutting out meant a big-time sin and the wrath of Mom, which could include the ultimate punishment—no surfing for a week.

This one Sunday, I dragged my heathen buddy Jon Sutherland to the 6 a.m. Mass. We were going surfing the minute church ended. About halfway through the Mass, this real small child in the pew in front of us—let's see, how do I say this nicely?—farted. Jon and I started to convulse with laughter. You know the feeling when you are not supposed to laugh and that is all you can do. We left church on the run because of uncontrollable laughter. If God ever asks me why I left church early, I had my excuse. I would blame the kid in front of us. We went surfing.

Honolulu

Honolulu was still a small town in the days of my youth. There were no shopping malls, no major highways, and everyone seemed to know each other. The Island's economy was percolating. The main business of Hawai'i was agriculture, with production of sugar and pineapple dominating the economy. Tourism was starting to take off. The development of regular jet airline flights around 1959 was the catalyst for the tourism boom. Now pineapple is gone, except for fields saved for tourist cameras and the few remaining sugar plantations' days are numbered.

All Ready for Kaukau *(food)*

Surfers are notorious chow hounds. We would surf for countless hours and then find as much food as possible for the least amount of money. Near Ala Moana was an eatery named Kapiolani Drive-In. This was in the days before fast foods. Kapiolani Drive-In had a special—five hamburgers for a dollar. The hamburgers would not win culinary awards. All they consisted of was a thin patty of hamburger and a bun and nothing else, not even butter…we would add catsup and each of us would eat five. That was our $1 lunch. The hamburgers would sit in our stomachs like cannonballs, forcing us into a semi-state of hibernation.

Rice

There were no exotic energy foods or high-performance drinks. Our energy food in Hawai'i was rice—still is. Primo beer was the high-energy beverage. Primo seemed to work better in the evening. Maruzens in Moili'ili served a *pipi* (beef) stew (mostly gravy) with a bucket of rice. If you wanted, you could get refills of rice till you were full. We did. Another favorite spot was a greasy spoon plate lunch stand named Yanai's. Yanai's had a few "specials," like fried bologna and rice, side of macaroni salad, or the island staple—fried spam, rice, side "mac" salad. Haleiwa featured Jerry's Sweet Shop as a pit stop (double entendre intended) for hungry surfers. Jerry's was torn down in 1978. Just as well—it would have fallen down. All plate lunches served with rice had a side scoop or two of macaroni salad that included enough mayonnaise to clog an elephant's arteries. Cholesterol was not in the vocabulary. The three major food groups in the Hawaiian diet are rice, macaroni salad and bread.

Breakfast of Champions

Try this health food breakfast to start your day—two eggs over easy on top of two scoops of rice and a double side of Portuguese sausage, all covered with catsup and...a side of two scoops "mac" salad, of course. Now, similar gourmet delights are called "loco moco."

Kaukau Contest

M's Ranch House was a family dining establishment. They staged a promotion that went like this. They would serve a 64-ounce steak (4 pounds), soup, a salad, vegetable, a whole baked potato, fruit punch or iced tea and a dessert. You would get the meal for free if you could eat it all in an hour or less. Buzzy Trent was the record holder. When M's Ranch House discontinued the wager, they said it was because surfers were wiping them out.

The Waikiki gang ate at the Sea View Inn or Joe's. Joe's was an interesting place, as it opened real early in the morning. Often there were beachboys on the way home from nocturnal maneuvers and beachboys up early to go surfing in the restaurant at the same time. The beachboys also frequented the Sands, an all-you-can-eat smorgasbord. It was conveniently right next to the Merry Go Round Bar. Incidentally, I observed at the Merry Go Round Bar that you don't ever want to drink at a bar that already is going around in a circle.

Summer Jobs

I worked every summer and kept 10 percent of my salary. The rest went to my family to help pay the bills. I did everything from being a surveyor's helper, or stacking heavy boxes of pineapples at the cannery, to being a beachboy. When I was 16, I got the all-time summer job—being a beachboy. My "boss" was the late James Koko. The entire beach services was run by Harry Robello, a handsome gentleman surfer of Portuguese ancestry—he gave me the job. What a job! After punching a time clock, I opened the concession up early every morning. The job consisted of renting surfboards to tourists and making sure they got back safely and on time. I "had" to paddle out into the surf often to make sure everything was OK. Sometimes I would be forced to catch waves before coming back in. Koko, my boss, seemed to understand.

What? Try Wait.

Communication can be curious in Hawai'i. Language changes. When I was a kid, there were fun terms that are not used much anymore. Here are a few of my favorite pidgin-English sayings:

Dig a toe—when you leave quickly, your toes dig in, especially if you are a barefooted kid in Hawai'i. So, when you wanted to leave somewhere quickly, you would say "dig a toe" out of here.

Hana bata days—you don't want to know the literal translation. "Hana bata days" basically means "snot nose kid" times.

Pearl dive—if the nose of your board dug in on the takeoff, you "pearl dived."

Coming down—you already know that it means "get out of the way—my wave."

Sliding right/sliding left—another warning for a surfer thinking of dropping in "sliding right"—in other words, "My wave and I am sliding your way, watch out."

Moke—basically means tough "local," but you don't want to use this term unless "you like beef."

You like beef?—do you want to fight? Never did figure out that one.

Pupule—means "crazy." Big wave riders are "pupule."

Da kine—my all-time favorite, it means anything you can't remember the word for, like:

Hey, der go da kine—means "there goes whoever."

I like kaukau da kine—means "I want to eat whatever."

No make the da kine—means "don't do that."
She get big da kine—means she has big eyes. Got you—I know what you were thinking.
Fricka—what polite local boys call you when they don't use the F... word.
Hot Curl—means getting a hot ride in the curl of the breaking wave.
Incidentally, speaking of old words and sayings, does anyone know where the word "gun" came from? How did big wave surfboards come to be named "guns"?

Can or No Can

Chubby Mitchell was a great surfer and friend. I love the guy. He often said, "If can, CAN, if no can, NO CAN." I think the Japanese say, *Shigata ga nai*. Some call it fate. Anyway, Chubby had it right on. That is the way it is.

Busted Because of B.A.

Speaking of California, we innocent Hawai'i kids heard that the California surfers had started a fad called "B.A.," also known rudely as "Bare Ass." This was the practice of hanging your bare bottom (*okole*) out in a public place. It also became known as "mooning." Well, at the time I was about 14 years old, and we trained for the canoe races at the Ala Wai near the yacht basin. On this infamous day, we drove back to the club in a pal's Volkswagen truck that had a canvas canopy over the back. My buddy Mike Sheehan rolled up the canvas and *forced* me, along with the others, to hang our little white fannies out the side of the van as we drove through Waikiki.

I happened to notice Reserve Police Officer Mossman in the car behind us as we drove up Kalakaua Ave. He was on the radio. We jumped out of the van and ran. The speed of our getaway was hampered by laughter. I turned the corner of a building and charged straight into the arms of a policeman—no longer funny. Mike Sheehan and another pal, Peter Guard, were apprehended, also. I was petrified. They hauled us down to the station and put us in a room where they put kids to scare them.

Sheehan walked in the station like he owned it and acted like an undercover cop just returning from a "sting operation." I was scared, but impressed by Mike Sheehan's boldness. Peter Guard and I were on the verge of tears, convinced that our lives had been ruined. For punishment my dad would send me to a Siberian slave camp. For having committed a mortal sin, my mother would probably enroll me in a monastery to cleanse my soul. The police let us stew in our fear for awhile.

We overheard them call my dad, who was once a reserve police officer. They knew him. The officer said, "Hey, Hemmings, come down and get your kid. We caught him hanging his ass out the side of a car in Waikiki." My parents confined me to home for one entire month of the summer. It was those darn California surfers that led us poor local boys astray.

Planning Ahead

Buzzy Trent, Fred Van Dyke and even Marge Calhoun and Marge Phillips lived in "surf" vans. This was way before anyone ever dreamed of recreation vehicles. When I was very young and infected with the surf fever, I planned my whole life. I drew a very detailed layout of my fantasy van that could accommodate two surfboards, a bed and a storage area. I made a detailed monthly budget. The way I had it planned, I could live the rest of my life surfing and living in the van for about $400 a month. The budget was right on, except I had not heard about inflation or taxes, (damn Democrats). Four hundred dollars would get you through a couple of days now. Just as well—I soon abandoned the plan.

Shucks, I had to grow up.

Catch a Wave

Location, Location, Location

I was standing on the beach at the Pipeline Masters, talking with Bill Flemming, the anchor commentator for *ABC Wide World of Sports*. At this point in my career, I was producing the event and also had been hired by ABC to be an "expert commentator." What many surfers did not realize in those early days of pro surfing was that the average Joe six-pack watching network television barely knew where the Hawaiian Islands were, much less anything about crazy surfers riding waves called Pipeline. Here was Bill Flemming wanting to be knowledgeable about the sport and asking a very simple question: "Why are the best waves in Hawai'i?"

It is a basic question. I gave him the long-winded answer: First, LOCATION. When you look at the globe, the Hawaiian Islands are sitting isolated in the middle of the largest expanse of open ocean in the world. There is a great deal of water and distance to work with. During the winter, huge, low-pressure storm systems travel across the North Pacific. Some of the storms are a thousand miles or more in size. These storms, like most everything else having to do with the

The Pipeline speaks— everyone pays attention.

weather, are difficult to predict. Sometimes storms grow, shrink away, stall or move sporadically. The point is that the storms, depending on their size and duration, create waves. Hawai'i is in the perfect location to catch the waves uninterrupted as they march into the Pacific. Bill Flemming asked, "Is that it?" Well...of course not, it gets very complicated on how the different forces of nature relate to the waves of Hawai'i. The North Shore of the island of O'ahu is facing the North Pacific almost perfectly. O'ahu, like all the Hawaiian islands, is the top of a very high and steep volcanic mountain range. The Hawaiian Islands are reposed on the ocean bed in deep water and receive the full impact of waves marching in the Pacific. Near shore reefs and beaches are sculpted as if some ancient Hawaiian god said, "I'm going to make the North Shore beaches perfect for surfing."

Bill Flemming and I talked on and on. Soon after, we went in front of the camera to do the "intro" to the show. Bill asked me that very question..."Why are the best waves in Hawai'i?" I gave him the short sound byte response and then he said something brilliant: "Thanks, Fred, and I bet those big winter storms that make these famous waves here on the North Shore of the island of O'ahu often move on to the continent and create great snow for skiers." He was right.

Waves

Surf Predictions – How Big, Rips, Death or Surviving, Fear and Dropping In.

It is always fun to hear the hard-core surf aficionados predicting waves. It sounds like this: Peter says, "Well, the swell is north by northwest, the interval is 11 and a half seconds, and the ground swell is 10 feet plus—sounds like the waves should be good at Sunset." Bernie interrupts, "Actually, Peter, I have a friend who got a phone call from his friend in a fishing boat on the way to Japan and he said the swell is 15 feet, with a 13-second interval and shifting to more northerly—sounds like we better head to

Waves have personalities—some are seductive and alluring, others are frightening.

Waimea." Then Ricky jumps in and says, "Hell, you guys, I saw the satellite photo that is only 38 minutes old that shows a large north swell 30-plus feet that will close out the North Shore an hour and 12 minutes from now and peak at 9:17 tonight —sounds like we better go surfing tomorrow."

Surf predictions, with the aid of satellites, ocean buoys, reports from vessels and smart meteorologists, are incredibly accurate. Dr. Roger Lucas of the University of Hawai'i can predict a winter swell within a couple of feet and hours. Intelligent predictions are even coming out of the southern hemisphere for summer surf. We get calls from Tahiti: "Hey, you guys, a big swell is hitting and headed your way." Talk about a long-distance indicator!! To think 30 years ago we would sometimes drive to the North Shore not knowing if it was 2 or 20 feet. We would always take a 9- to10-foot small wave board and our 11- to 12-foot gun for a big swell.

How Big Is That Wave?

Here is an argument as old as surfing: How big is that wave? Corky Carroll called me in 1969 and wanted a contribution to an article he was compiling for *Surfer Magazine*. Here is what I gave him.

Judging wave size

published in *Surfer Magazine,* 1969
Surfer Tips No. 92

Judging wave size is often a disputed issue, especially here in Hawaii where the size of waves varies so drastically. In the larger surf one of the more difficult problems is determining what exactly the baseline to start the measurement from, since the trough of the wave is so long and slopping. Scientific measurement of wave size is very accurate for scientific purposes, but not for surfing. Generally, it would be safe to measure a wave from the lowest point on the face of the wave that a surfer can ride to the top of the crest. It is important to emphasize that pictures are a total waste of time, as every different angle gives a different perspective of the wave.

The intelligent and knowledgeable surfer therefore measures a wave with an "educated guesstimate" which for all intents and purposes is fairly accurate in surf up to 20 feet. Since our experience is limited in surf much over 20 feet it is hard to put an exact numerical figure on the size of waves in this category. Maybe it would be better to measure surf at this level in increments of fear rather than feet.

39

That is how it appeared in *Surfer Magazine* around 30 years ago. The debate of judging wave size continues to this day. I understand that some are now saying that the real way to measure a wave is from the back. So, we have a front measurement and a back measurement to argue over. Personally, I feel measuring a wave from the back is like having a beauty contest and only looking at the contestants' rear ends. What I do know is that the farther you get from Hawai'i, the bigger the waves seem to get. An 8-foot wave on the North Shore is often 12-plus somewhere else.

I guess that is because Hawaiian feet are bigger.

Rip Currents

Swells in the ocean are not moving water, just the energy is moving. This is similar to a wave that can be created when you jerk up and down on a long rope stretched between two points. When swells get to shore and become breaking waves, then the water starts to move. The more and the bigger the waves, the more water is being pushed to shore. The water seeks its level and returns to sea in what is called rip currents. On big days the rip current can be so strong you cannot paddle your board against it. Each site has its own rip current pattern. When the surf is small, there is little or no rip current. When the surf is up, unsuspecting neophytes can get caught in the rip current and end up getting rescued or worse.

Death

What a terrible heading for a story from my surfing past. When I grew up, there was no explicit violence in the media and I guess we all were less sensitized and accommodating to the ugliness and sorrows of death.

I was 12 years old in 1958, when I finally talked my dad into driving me to the North Shore to surf. I thought I could handle Haleiwa. We drove up

Surfers stroking into a monstrous wave don't think of death, though their hearts race, breath is short and body is tense with fear. Sometimes the man dies before the wave. Mark Foo rides eternity as a legend of surfing.

and got out of the car just in time to see the fire rescue team bringing in a drowned surfer. I had never seen a dead person. It was traumatic. I couldn't comprehend the limp, dead body of what minutes before had been a handsome young surfer. It gave me nightmares.

Death stalked me on a few occasions during my reckless days of riding big waves. You really never think about dying on a bad wipeout. You are too busy fighting to survive. On a close out day at Paumalu one year, I wiped out and somehow ended up in no man's land between the point and the outside lineup. I was trapped in a current that was running out and under the incoming waves. It was freaky. I would dive under 15-foot walls of white water and then fight back to the surface to find myself stuck in the same place. The water under the waves was pulling out and the water near the surface was moving in with the force of the waves. After a few soundings, I began to panic. The waves were huge and cruel. I was so scared my diaphragm was stuck high in my chest. I could not even get a good breath. I realized what was happening and, if I continued to dive under the waves and try to swim in between them, I would die. I decided to take the next wave on the surface, where the water was moving in to the safety of shore. I went limp and took the full impact of the propelling mountain of water. The mantra of big wave wipeouts is "relax" and save oxygen till the force of the wave subsides enough to move toward safety. It worked. There are times in life when you stop fighting in order to survive.

Big Surf Survival

Big wave riders are a different breed. They constitute a very small portion of all surfers. One thing that sets them apart is that they know deep in their conscious that huge surf can kill you. Big wave riders live in constant fear of that wipeout that might take away the breath of life. They often hide the fear behind a mask of machismo. Wipeout skills are important to learn. I wrote Surfer Tip No.19 in the mid-sixties for *Surfer Magazine*.

Big Wave Survival
Surfer Tip No. 19

Take it from me, every surfer fears the big wave wipe out. The surfer who says he doesn't is either a fool or a liar. Even so the thrills bring back experienced surfers every winter to challenge and conquer Hawaii's big surf. How do they do it?

First the big wave rider is experienced and in great physical condition—an excellent swimmer who has developed his breathing capacity for bad wipeouts.

Most of all he knows his own capabilities and tries not to pit his surfing skills against an unbeatable wave.

A word about Hawaii's big surf. Every winter off the north shore of the island of Oahu the biggest rideable waves in the world are produced by storms in the Northern Pacific. These storms create large ground swells traveling in the direction the wind is blowing. Coming out of the North Pacific they hit the North Shore with particular force because there's no continental shelf to drag and tax their energies. These swells break with the power that could snap a 11-foot surfboard like a match stick or push a surfer 40 feet down and bounce him off a jagged coral bottom. Riding these waves is a challenging and tricky business and there is no room for the inexperienced.

Even the old pros have their tricks. While paddling out on a big day at Waimea, Australian Bob Pike takes a few dives to adjust to the water and the pressure changes. Perhaps Pike was impressed by George Downing's story about diving under a huge Makaha wave and coming up with a ruptured ear drum.

Incidentally, George Downing has a unique way of bailing out when he sees a wipe out coming. George kicks his board out from under him and lands on his seat. in the water. While this may get a laugh later at a surfing movie, it is smart and functional. By kicking his board away George cuts his chance of getting hit by it and landing on his wax pocket slows him down and softens the impact. By contrast a surfer who flat dives off his board on a big wave frequently skips down the face like a rock on a small pond. This surfer may end up in the most powerful part of the breaking wave.

Greg Noll who has stuffed himself into more than his share of 25 foot waves, tries to have as much oxygen as possible when he faces an inevitable wipeout. Greg, like many other surfers, realizes that sprinting to pick up a big wall burns oxygen and consumes energy two things really needed when you are held down on a wipeout. So when Greg paddles for a wave he breathes deeply in and out a few times (hyper-ventilates). This pumps in as much oxygen as possible.

A big wave wipeout means a surfer is held down 10 or 12 seconds before the power of the wave dissipates and he can battle up through the white water. A dozen seconds may not seem long to be under the water but a surfer who's used up most of his oxygen and energy paddling for the wave, sliding down its face and then getting boiled- those few seconds can seem like an eternity. Anyone who thinks twelve seconds isn't a long time is correct, but try jumping into a thrashing, tearing breaking ocean and see how long you can hold your breath.

Don't panic is the advice given to surfers facing a big wipeout-but frequently this advice is hard to follow. Every experienced surfer knows not to fight the churning wave because he cannot overcome its force. He knows, too, that if he relaxes and waits, the wave will release him. But even the experienced surfers hit the panic button on bad wipeouts when they are held down so long that the basic animal instinct for self preservation takes over. Then it's wild clawing for the surface and that precious lung full of air.

Sometimes being tossed and turned under a mountain of white water can leave a surfer greatly confused in the sense of swimming direction. Fred Van Dyke tells of the time when he thought he was scratching for the surface but actually swam into the bottom. The next time Fred wiped out, he opened his eyes and swam for the light and the surface.

Paul Gebauer, another alert wave rider, holds his nose on a wipeout (note SURFER TIPS Vol. 5&6). This conserves Paul's lung full of air instead of some escaping inadvertently through his nose. Paul notices that the body automatically blows air out the nose to prevent water from being pushed into the sinuses and lungs.

One other tip: When a surfer comes up after a bad wipeout, he should take a few deep breaths to pump back some of the oxygen he's burned while he was held down..

These are a few of the techniques the big wave riders use when they are challenging the big surf—surfers who know the ocean and their own capabilities. Unlike inexperienced surfers, they never go out on a day they feel they don't belong. They are the surfers who, with each wave, gain more and more knowledge about surviving the big wave wipeout.

I just noticed while retyping this article from 30 years ago that it is done entirely in the masculine. That is not too politically correct nowadays. This gives me the idea to take up later in this book the notion that surfing is a macho sport. One thing I do know is that women are capable of riding big surf and have not. It will happen.

We'll talk about it later.

Be careful stroking into a monster wave that will surely punish you, play the odds. No guts no glory doesn't mean suicide.

The Fear Line

This past winter I sneaked out to Makaha early one January morning. The surf was about 12 to 15 feet off the point. I had my stiletto big wave board. When I reached the point, there were only a few local guys out. Makaha still seems to be the best-kept secret in surfing. Anyway the surf was only 12 to 15, like I said. Twenty years ago, I would have surfed with reckless abandon. A 15-foot wave really can't do much damage. Well, I was hesitant and, yes, fear made me cautious. Seems my fear line has dropped considerably. I used to surf big point waves and didn't really get scared till it was bigger than 15 feet. Everyone has a fear line, and it changes.

The Zone

The zone is what they call it now. Distance runners call it "runner's high." We are finding out that in the realm of intense pursuits our bodies produce endorphins, or a self-induced natural high, the "zone." It happens in surfing. Though in the past I did not realize what was happening, it is now coming into focus. Entering the Zone can be part of the surfing adventure. For some, the zone is so euphoric that they feel that surfing is some sort of a religious experience.

Surfers can sometimes remember waves from 30 or more years ago like they just kicked out. Years ago, a unique sand bar washed in at Pupukea. A 6-foot shore break walled across the sand bar, forming incredibly hollow, but safe, tubes. Something happened to me that day. Without conscious effort, I could do no wrong. Surfing without inhibitions, I found myself doing things and going places on the waves of Pupukea that seemed impossible. That day at Pupukea I took off on this one wave and climbed high as it walled up, and, falling, I started to dart across the face of the wave. It seemed like I was riding in slow motion. The curl of the break hit me right in the middle of my head, as I crouched at the bottom of the wave. I should have wiped out. As if time were on my side, I leaned to the inside rail of the board and pulled up the face of the wave into a crystal chamber. It lasted several fleeting seconds. I guess I hit the zone. Surfers know the feeling.

This was the "zone" day on the Pupukea sand bar. It was magical.

Dropping In

Dropping in is bad manners. The etiquette is that the surfer who catches the wave first or has the curl position has the right of way. This is an unwritten safety rule of everyday surfing, and it is a very strictly enforced rule in competitive surfing. Dropping in is taking off in front of a surfer with wave priority. Sometimes in bigger waves, where skillful surfers rocket across the face of massive walls of water and don't maneuver much, there is room for two and even three surfers to ride together. We live in a crowded world and certainly most surf sites are too packed, especially here in Hawai'i. Dropping in can be hazardous and sometimes leads to altercations. Never drop in on a big, tough guy who can kick your *okole*, because he probably will.

Common sense is not in the rule book of life.
Be cool on the North Shore.

45

Barefoot Tour

Cruise with me to the surfs I know and love.

The West Side

The west coast of O'ahu is positioned to capture the north swells of the winter, as well as the south swells of the summer.

In the days of my youth, the drive to the west side was a journey. A two-lane road weaved its way from Honolulu out through Aiea and Waipahu, the plantation town surrounded by sugar cane fields, over the plain of 'Ewa around Barbers Point, to the western shores now called the Waianae or "leeward" coast. Nanakuli, Maili and Waianae were little towns on the west side.

Maili

On rare occasions we would end up paddling out at Maili, rather than motoring down the coast to Makaha. Maili was forever altered by the U.S. Army Corps of Engineers when the adjacent stream was turned into a monstrosity storm drain. The huge boulder breakwater altered the surf. I sure hope we learn from our mistakes.

Makaha

Makaha is a special place for me. My surfing life is overflowing with memories of Makaha—so much so that the next chapter is MAKAHA.

Keawaula — *Otherwise Known as Yokohama*

Have you ever wondered why a beautiful Hawaiian beach would be called Yokohama Bay? For the first half of the twentieth century, a railroad ran from the Iwilei depot at downtown Honolulu out to the Waianae coast, and around Kaena Point, all the way to Kahuku. The train would sometimes stop near a famous Hawaiian beach and area named Keawaula. The train would let off and pick up Japanese fishermen. The beach soon gained the nickname of Yokohama because of the Japanese fishermen. The south swell surfing is as good as the fishing. The break is called Yokohama, too. Too bad the railroad was closed. It would have been perfect for surf journeys, among other things. Interestingly, the North Shore jogging path is built on the old railway line. Honolulu could really use a ready-made mass transit corridor, like the "Magic Island" debacle that is politics. I'll talk more about politics and surfing later.

In the early days of my surfing life we often traveled to Makaha, or, in the summer, to Keawaula. We shared the bountiful waves with friends on the Waianae coast. Good fun.

48

Keawaula was happening on this summer day in 1965. Photographer Phil Wilson caught two basic moods. On the left "casual." On the right "uptight."

The North Shore

There is probably more energy generated in one day of big surf on the North shore than a month's worth of surfing anywhere else. The North Shore is the undisputed mecca of the surfing world. The overused metaphor is that the North Shore is the Dr. Jekyll and Mr. Hyde of surfing. During the summer, in the absence of winter swells, the ocean is tranquil. The personality of the fabled coast metamorphoses in the winter, when swells can turn into killer surf within hours. The coastline from Haleiwa to Paumalu is the most famous surfing venue in the world. It is the big league of surfing.

Haleiwa

Henry Preece was the reigning *ali'i* of Haleiwa in the fifties and early sixties. Like Buffalo, this guy is a classic, with a heart full of aloha. One of Henry's best surfing buddies is the *haole moke*, Greg Noll. I have heard rumors that they have consumed more than a few beers together.

You used to have to drive down the coast from Sea View Inn, and double back on an always muddy road through a jungle of *haole koa* and weeds to view the waves. Now, the same area is a vast park. Some say the lefts are good—I never believed it. On an 8- to 10-foot day, there is nothing like pulling up high into the face of a Haleiwa wave. It is a speed ride. Because of volumes of water rushing in from Avalanche outside the Haleiwa break on a big day, there is a constant rip current running through the lineup. Sometimes the rip is so strong you have to paddle continually to stay in the lineup.

The town of Haleiwa was once a little resort and plantation village on the O'ahu railway line. The Haleiwa hotel graced the shores of Anahulu stream. Now, the sugar industry is dead and the resort hotel, like the O'ahu railway, is long since gone. Haleiwa is the world's surfing capital. The town is littered with surf-related business. Surfing is the industry of the North Shore. During the winter, surfers from all over the world use Haleiwa town as their base.

Laniakea

Laniakea is a fantastic, long, heavy-duty right slide when the swell is from the northeast and big. By the way, when you are standing facing the ocean on the North Shore, a north swell coming out of the Kaena Point direction is a "northwest" swell. Swells coming form the Kahuku direction are "northeast" swells. Laniakea is best on a northeast swell, interestingly enough most often early in the winter surf season.

Every once in awhile, on a west swell, a huge left slide called **Himalayas** breaks. We rode it several times. The difficulty at Himalayas was that, if you lost your board, it was about three-fourths of a mile swim to shore. A board would go all the way in and sometimes drift back out in the rip running between Himalayas and Laniakea.

Chuns Reef

Sally Hodgins and I were wrestling. Our pals—Toni, Nina and Margi—piled on when I started to win. We were high school kids drinking beer on Chun's Reef beach and having fun. Back in the early sixties you could do things like that and not get busted.* These girls were like my sisters in high school. They were all too smart to be anything more. We were buddies.

Chun's Reef, when the beach is partially washed out, has a freshwater spring that creates a crystal-clear pool in the rocks by the water's edge. We would surf the fun waves all day and then use the pool to cool and rinse off. Amazingly, sometimes there would be Primo beer in the spring. Just another part of this paradise, Hawai'i. Oh, the waves at Chun's are play waves. It closes out at about 6 to 8 feet.

I didn't surf much at Chun's, because I didn't have to. If the waves were good there, they were usually better at Haleiwa, Pupukea or small Sunset. You could pretty much surf where you wanted to, when you wanted.

*Public service announcement...**do not drink and drive**. Having a few beers and wrestling lovely young ladies on the beach is OK.

Waimea Bay

Huge Waimea waves had put a thin veil of salt spray in the still morning air. It was 1974 and the Smirnoff contest was on hold. The surf, 25 feet-plus. It was the biggest Waimea surf I had seen that was still rideable. Peter Cole came running up to me as we were setting up the scaffolding for the event and pleaded that I not send contestants out. It was too big. If Peter Cole was scared, you can imagine what everyone else felt like. Soon I was surrounded by Mark Richards, Reno Abellira and a handful of contestants who were agreeing with Peter. It was too big. Just then, a set exploded in the lineup. The waves, when hitting shore, literally washed up and over the beach into the small park. I was on the spot. Hold the contest in the best big surf ever or cancel. I knew that it could be an historic event. My decision—"dead ahead"—let's run the contest. I pulled the greatest bluff of my surfing life. I looked at the pro surfers

Eddie Aikau watched as I fell into this Waimea wall in the winter of 1967. The vapor trail on the takeoff is caused by my board going airborne. The splashdown almost buckled my knees. I made it to the bottom of the wave and promptly got stuffed—big time. I am sure Eddie knew where I was bound for on the takeoff. Tim McCollough, now CEO of Reyn's Spooner Company, took the photo.

and said, "If I go out and successfully ride a wave, the contest is on, OK???" They looked at me in horror. I guess they figured if Fred Hemmings goes out and we don't, it will look like we choked. The surfers reluctantly agreed to compete. It ended up being the most epic big wave contest. P.S. I probably would NOT have gone out if the surfers had called my bluff. It was too big.

Waimea Bay is one of the most renowned big wave venues in the world. It put big wave surfing on the map back in the sixties. The first mountain men of Waimea are legendary. Buzzy Trent, Jose Angel, Greg Noll and Max Lim were among the trailblazers. Ken Bradshaw, James Jones, Derrick Doerner, Brock Little and a number of other big wave specialists carry on the tradition.

In December of 1994 Mark Foo, who weaned his big wave mastery at Waimea, surfed into forever with his untimely death while riding huge waves at a spot in California named Mavericks. Mark was in pursuit of his life's passion. Was the wave that killed him at Mavericks his fate?

My greatest Waimea memories are of Eddie. Eddie Aikau and I were contemporaries surfing together at Waimea. We were friends who rode the waves.

Pipeline

It was 1960. I had caught a ride to the North Shore with my big brother Butchie, a great surfer. Tim Guard, the 1957 Makaha junior champion, was with us. We pulled up to the parking lot at Pupukea. No one was out, it was

This Pipeline wave almost killed me. It was 1966 and I was on the way in from a boring session of waiting for waves on the second reef. I caught this thick inside wave on my "Blue Max." I ended up framed on the wall of water like a tortured victim on a medieval rack. The wipeout pinned me on the bottom. I broke the surface just as the next wave hit. I almost drowned.

closed-out surf. We looked down the beach toward Kaena Point and saw, to our astonishment, a 10-foot tube, breaking like a machine-made monster. What the heck is that? we wondered. We raced down the coast, parked the car and walked in with our boards. I paddled out and, probably by the luck of the ignorant, made it through the shore break with no trouble. I paddled into what appeared to be the lineup, and waited. A set came and I swung my 9-foot-plus "hot dog" board (now considered a tanker) around to take off. After a few strokes, I was sucked to the top of the wave. Plummeting down the face, I am sure I pulled a few Gs trying to bottom turn. The wall of water caved in. The wipeout was like the US Navy had just rolled a depth charge in the ocean. I literally exploded back to the surface. The rip was racing along the beach faster than my brother could run to keep up with me. I made it to shore. My brother yelled and screamed at me words to the effect that, if I had died, Dad would have killed him. My brother had his priorities right. Several years later, Phil Edwards rode the break and the site acquired the name of Pipeline. Phil was the first modern-day surfer to successfully ride the Pipeline. My brother Butchie and Tim Guard will attest that I got the first modern-day wipeout. I was lucky. Actually, I am sure Pipeline had been the source of surfing adventures for the ancient Hawaiians.

The Pipeline is probably the most famous wave in all of surfing. I like to say that it breaks with the precision of a guillotine. The swell jumps up on the shallow reef and pitches out to form a perfect tube. Pipeline has created heroes and tragically taken lives.

Pupukea

Off Ke Nui Road in the *hau* trees was a little parking area that could hold about five cars. We were sitting on the edge of the *hau* trees at the top of the steep incline to the beach, watching the fun sand bar break named Pupukea. With a roar, an old, beat-up surfmobile drove up and three road warrior young men literally jumped out of the windows. Remember, the early sixties were prim and proper times. Even surfers dressed neatly. Well, these guys jumping out of the car were wild-looking and unshaven, wore tank shorts and what looked like rags, which were tucked into the waist, hanging down, Indian-style. They barked with an accent. It was the first time I had encountered Australian surfers on the North Shore. I could not figure the Australian surfers out—some seemed to be driven by genetic forces I don't understand. We all surfed Pupukea that day and had fun. It was crowded—there must have been six surfers out. Pupukea, like Chun's Reef, was a fun break we played in.

"Alii arch" bottom turn at Paumalu, 1965— known now as the "soul arch."

Paumalu – *Sunset Beach*

Let's return Hawai'i to Hawaiian places. Paumalu is the Hawaiian name of the area now called Sunset Beach. Paumalu has such a romantic and colorful legacy from old Hawai'i.

Paumalu is one of the premier breaks in the surfing world and has been the battleground for many famed competitions. It has been the venue for surfing's ultimate contests—the Duke, Smirnoff, World Cup and the Excel.

The north and westerly swells hit the reef in such a manner that the peak seems to shift. The wave breaks hard and fast. It is a tricky spot. The famous "rip" at Paumalu gathers momentum near the shore and then heads straight out the channel. Before it leashes, the rip could take a board back out before a surfer could swim in, occasionally resulting in lost boards.

Paumalu is one of surfing's preferred stages. Some of the players from my era have worn the moniker of "Mr. Sunset." Favorites include Barry Kanaiapuni, Tiger Espere and Jeff Hakman.

I have written this section of my book about the North Shore and the surfing sites that I frequented in my heyday, 30 years ago. I've just realized we never surfed many of the sites on the North Shore being ridden now. Let's see—Gas Chambers, Back Door, Back Yards, Kammie Land, Pinball's—the list is long. One of the great joys of surfing in the sixties is that it was seldom crowded. We didn't have to seek out secondary surf sites. We were already surfing the best.

Maui — *wowie*

The Prince Kuhio Day celebration on Maui in 1959 included the Kahului Harbor outrigger canoe races. In those days, travel was much less extensive and I had barely been interisland and had never ventured beyond the shores of Hawai'i. The weekend trip to Maui was a big deal. I was traveling with paddling buddies as part of the 13-years-old-and-under crew. The Outrigger Canoe Club also sent an "open" team of our best paddlers. Our Maui hosts were, in the finest local style, most gracious. The day after the race, Bobby Meheula, a woman surfing pioneer on Maui, said the Maui surfers would pick us up and take us to a new "secret" spot.

In 1963 I spent the day surfing Honolua bay with a friend—yes, only one friend to share the waves.

Today Honolua Bay gets crowded—too crowded.

We threw boards in the back of a flatbed truck, piled in a few cars and started on a long ride on an old two-lane road from Kahului to Lahaina. Lahaina was a sleepy little town with one hotel, the Pioneer Inn. The only thing of note at Ka'anapali was the graveyard. The way from there on was a dirt road. We drove past several of the six famous bays of Hono a Pi'ilani. Coming around the bend high on a hill we saw, peeling off the far side of a bay, 6-foot, perfect waves. We had arrived at the secret spot, Honolua Bay. We surfed till we were exhausted and could barely carry our boards back up the cliff.

I took several trips in the succeeding years to surf Honolua. On one trip, pals Buzzy Lee, Buzzy Knuebuhl and I were guests at a Punahou classmate Roger Berg's house. It was Easter break. His father, Karl Berg, was manager of the Pioneer Sugar Plantation. That was a big deal, because back then sugar was still king in the Hawai'i economy. We lived in the comfort of the Berg's grand home on the shores of Lahaina. My pal Buzzy Lee had eyes for Roger's sister Busey. That is another story that I promised Buzzy I would not detail. Every morning we would pack lunches and Mrs. Berg would drop us off at Honolua Bay to surf. She would pick us up usually late in the afternoon. We surfed waves varying from 2 feet to 6 feet all week long. Only once in awhile would someone show up to surf. We rode waves conservatively, because there was no such thing as a leash. At Honolua the waves wash up onto the rocks. One day a friend lost his board in front of the cave. It came out in pieces the next day. Can you imagine surfing Honolua Bay for a week with no one out but a few pals??? Should have been there.

Kauai – *The Separate Kingdom*

Kaua'i is sometimes referred to as "the separate kingdom," because Kamehameha the Great, who conquered the Islands to create the Kingdom of Hawai'i, never conquered Kaua'i. It is a unique island.

Nowadays, Hanalei Bay is a getaway place for celebrities and a handful of surf legends like Billy Hamilton, Jeff Hakman and Peter Pope Kahapea. The point wave at Hanalei is potent. It's a cross between Makaha and Laniakea when it is big—at 10 feet, with the right direction, surfing Hanalei will make you feel like you've died and gone to...Hanalei...I mean, heaven.

Kaua'i is pregnant with great surf sites.

The Big Island

Paul Strauch and I spent several days in the mid sixties on the Big Island of Hawai'i, searching for surf. At the time, there were only a few regular surfers there. We surfed Honoli'i on the Hilo side of the island and then rode the waves of Banyans in Kona. I have just returned from a nostalgia event at Banyans. Some of the old-timers from the sixties attended. The waves haven't change. We sure have.

Now, the Big Island surfers know all the spots and when to hit them. Curiously, with a limited population, the Big Island has a disproportionate number of young guns on the pro tour. The Big Island boys are hot.

What is really neat about the Big Island is the ancient Hawaiian sites. At Kahalu'u on the Kona coast there is a small surf that breaks outside an ancient *heiau* (shrine). Kuemanu is a surfing *heiau*. The gods of nature in ancient Hawai'i included special gods for the ocean and surf. It gave real meaning to the term "pray for surf," because that is what happened at Kuemanu Heiau.

57

These were the surfs of the Hawai'i I grew up in. Hawai'i No Ka Oi...

Makaha

I am convinced that there are many forces at work in our universe that we have not really "discovered" yet. Have you ever noticed that certain areas, sites and neighborhoods just plain make you comfortable? There is a hidden magnetism to places that we are comfortable at. I am comfortable at Makaha. I always have felt at home at Makaha. Of course, the Keaulanas, Rell, the Desotos, Homer and his family, and all my friends at Makaha have contributed to the comfort level. Comfort is often created by more than the obvious. Makaha is special. Where else can "*menehune* children" be surfing in gentle, 2-foot surf one day and the next day the waves can be 20 feet high—striking fear into the hearts of the bravest of big wave riders? That's Makaha. Where else on a fun day can you have waves that accommodate a body surfer, boogie boarder, a tandem team of maybe three or four surfers riding in an outrigger canoe? That's Makaha.

After countless waves and eons of fun, I am intimate with Makaha. I know her. On small days, inside waves peel off the reef. Makaha waves have soft shoulders. Surfers are often catapulted into the air, as the famous Makaha backwash forms a wave returning to the sea after washing up the steep beach. On 8-foot-plus days, the waves move out past an area in midbay called the Blow Hole. The special days are "Point Surf," which I still contend is the best big wave in the world.

59

Riding Makaha Point Surf

I learned to dance with the waves of Makaha like a child learning the piano—practice, practice and more practice. The good part is that practice consisted of surfing, surfing and more surfing. I know Makaha.

On big surf days the lineup is outside the famous Beall home, directly on the point. The Makaha waves are best on north or northwest swells. The swell bends or "wraps" around Kaena Point and marches down the coast to Makaha. At most surf sites you look for a set out on the horizon and then scramble to meet it. The trick at Makaha is to look right up the coast from the point. The huge sets can be seen about a mile away toward Kaena Point before they can be seen looming on the horizon. That gives a smart surfer a little head start. When sitting in the lineup on a point day with a group of surfers, I used to always try and position myself outside the pack. When I saw a set coming, I would fade to the right, paddling out. The pack would usually cover. At the last moment I would cut abruptly back to the left to safely take off on the wave I wanted.

On the takeoff of a point wave, you can often calculate real quickly whether you are bound for glory or a wipeout by how the wall lines up into the bay. I always calculate in my mind the odds of making a wave by percentage—in other words, I would surmise, this is a 50–50 wave, or this is an open door with a 75 percent chance of making it. Gambling on the waves slightly against being successfully ridden is where to find the challenge. Proning out or trying to lie down and hang on a wave over 15 feet is futile. Usually on a point wave you can angle for the top of the wave in what is called the "saddle" and get out before the notorious bowl. In larger surf, I always count waves in the set and very rarely opt for the first couple of waves. I do not want to confront the subsequent walls of water in case of a wipeout or late kickout in the saddle.

The bowl, depending on the slight subtleties in the swell direction, would present the real challenge of riding point surf at Makaha. With an unfavorable swell direction, the bowl will break before you get there. Usually it is a close call. A way to beat a close call is to gain as much altitude on the face of the wave before the bowl and then use your falling speed to race through the bowl. If you are gutsy and a chance taker, speed gained by altitude could propel you out and around the breaking white water. Prepare to get your *okole* kicked if you miscalculate. An explosive wipeout at the "bowl" is the price surfers must sometimes pay for the thrill of riding big surf at Makaha.

The waves of Makaha are classic.

People, through the years, have asked me what my favorite surf is. Well, that is like asking Greg Noll or Buffalo what their favorite food is. I like to surf wherever the waves are, but I guess I do have a favorite surf…MAKAHA.

Makaha International Surfing Championships

The Makaha Championships was the contest that laid the foundation for international competition. The event was a labor of love for the Waikiki Surf Club. The surfers who worked so hard in the early days of the Makaha event to make it a reality included Wally Froiseth and his wife, Moku, John Lind, Rudy Choy, Russ Takaki, Johnny McMahon, Dougie Forbes, David Klausemeyer and Clarence Maki, among others. The first event in 1954 was an immediate success. Chinn Ho, the famous businessman who had interests in developing Makaha Valley, contributed substantially to the event. Community organizations in Waianae, like the Lions Club, helped out. Even friends from Lima, Peru, such as Poncho Weise and Edwardo Arena and Les Williams of California would show up in Hawaiʻi and assist with officiating the Makaha Championships.

The participants and winners of the Makaha Championships read like a list of the who's who of the sport of surfing. Rabbit Keikai, Allen Gomes, Walter Hoffman, Ethel Kukea, George Downing, Conrad Canha, Peter Cole, Marge Calhoun, Jamma Keikai, Nappy Napoleon, Mud Warner, Buffalo Keaulana and Linda Benson are listed as finalists and winners at Makaha in the very early years of the competition.

The Makaha International Surfing Championships was actually a water sports carnival. Events included women's open, senior open and junior men championships, bodysurfing, paddleboard races, tandem surfing and, for several years, they even held "mat" surfing competition. "Mats" were inflatable mattress-like vehicles a little longer than a modern belly board. Filled with compressed air, they became rigid. I can't recall who the "mat" surfing champions were, though I know several guys who claim to be the nocturnal "mat" tandem surfing champions.

Down through the years the Makaha Championships judges refined competitive rules. I upset my older brother and his friends because of an archaic rule in 1958. I was 12 years old in the Under 18 Years Old Junior Men's division. I survived the prelims and was in the finals with what must have been 12 other surfers. There was no interference rule. The scoring was, as I said, antiquated. Every wave ridden would be scored and all waves for each contestant would be added together to determine the winner. It did not take me long to figure out quantity could beat quality. The waves for the finals were about 8 feet, breaking out in the blow hole lineup. I was 12 years old and too chicken to go all the way out to the "big" waves. I stayed in and caught what must have been 20 low-scoring waves. Strategy seemed to be my competitive edge throughout most of my athletic career.

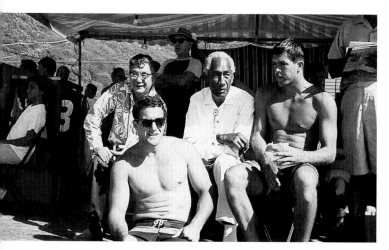

Butch Van Artsdalen and I joined business tycoon Chinn Ho and surfing legend Duke Kahanamoku for a break at the 1965 Makaha Contest.

The big guys were really mad at me because I rode small inside waves to outscore many of them in the finals of the 1958 Junior Men's competition. (l to r) The winner was Nappy Napoleon, second—Paul Strauch, third—the small kid, fourth—Don Stroud and fifth—Wayne Miyata.

I rode one of the first Hobie foam boards in Hawai'i in the prelims of the 1958 contest.

I'll concede that this strategy was based on a flawed rule. My brother and his pals surfed outside and got a few high-scoring waves apiece. I ended up in third place behind Nappy Napoleon and Paul Strauch. I remember thinking—well, I played by the "rules" and beat those old guys. They didn't agree. Rightfully so, the rule changed the following year.

Something happened every day at the Makaha Championships. Surfers would report in or listen to the radio at about 7:30 every morning, when the decision on what event would be held was made depending on the surf. The contest was staged over the Christmas holidays. Literally thousands of spectators—six, seven, eight-people deep—would be on the beach. There was entertainment, food concessions and even night torch surfing. The Makaha International Surfing Championships were special.

After years of continuous surfing at Makaha, business, family and life in general took me on different adventures. I no longer surfed Makaha regularly. A big swell beckoned after years of retirement from being a devout regular. I wrote about the surf session in an article published by the Outrigger Canoe Club monthly magazine and *Surfing Magazine*. Here it is:

The Legendary Waves of Makaha – *published in 1982*

There is no place in the world like Makaha when it is right. Over the years the emphasis in surfing has focused on pros ripping apart small to moderate surf. Big Makaha is more of a legend than a reality to most contemporary surfers. The "point"

Makaha wave is a huge aqua blue wall that lines up and rifles a surfer for a ride of over a quarter mile. Few contemporary surfers have had the experience of riding the point on a big day.

This was the cast of semi-finalists in the 1965 contest, quite a lineup. (l to r) Fred, Buffalo, Steve Bigler, Dewey Weber, George Downing, Paul Strauch, Joey Cabell, Rick Steere, Kiki Spangler, unidentified, Ben Aipa, brother Mark Hemmings and Mike Doyle. Thirty plus years later we are all still chasing waves.

February 17, early in the morning, Karl Heyer, a young surfer and canoe paddler from the Outrigger Canoe Club, called to say Joe Teipel was reporting that the North Shore was being battered by damaging surf. North and West beaches were closed by the civil defense. It didn't take us longer than half a second to decide that Makaha is where it would be happening.

Karl was in an executive training program with a long established and prominent Hawaiian company. Only in Hawai'i can a 25 year old go up to his boss and ask permission to go surfing because the waves were big. Karl's boss gave him the pass and we were off and running. It brought immediate flashbacks of similar journeys in the sixties...we were headed for huge Makaha.

The surf was thundering, a solid, glassy 15 to 20 feet. No one was out. The beach had completely washed away, and the bath house was once again precariously balanced on its foundation. We were soon on the long paddle out to the channel, where we stopped to take a few dives to acclimate our bodies and lungs, then over to the point.

Once on the point, it was my misfortune to rush into the first wave. The wave in the vicinity of 20 feet lined up like the great wall of China. I made the classic mistake. Rather than angling down the wall right on the take off, I dropped into a

Makaha Scrapbook

George Downing was my mentor. We often competed against each other, too. George is recognized as one of the great pioneers of the early days of surfing at Makaha.

Even though I am making a left-turn signal, I am turning right.

On the nose in the Junior Men's finals in 1963.

My shirt said 0—I placed better in the 1964 contest.

And in this corner, weighing too much, in the white trunks—Rocky Hemmoroids. I don't like this 1964 photo because I look like an old boxer. The reason I am including the picture is so you can see the scoreboard that utilized a very complicated judging system.

The 1963 Makaha finalists included Senior Men's: (top, l to r) Buffalo Keaulana—third, Rabbit Kekai—second, George Downing—Champion. In the Junior Men's division: Barry Kanaiapuni—third, Fred Hemmings—first and Eric Romanchek—second.

bottom turn. The extra split seconds would make it impossible to complete the wave and sure enough, about half way down the line the wave threatened to cave in on me. Angling for the top to get out, the lip grabbed the board and I was launched into the air. I came down just in the right position to be pulled over the falls backwards.

It was my first 20 foot wave wipeout in years. Both my contacts popped out, my sinuses were douched by what seemed like the entire Pacific ocean and once again I realized how vulnerable a surfer is in huge waves. It was a long swim in. Walking up the beach to retrieve my board, I was not to sure I wanted to go out again. It was the first round and I had already been KO'd.

Hesitantly paddling back out around the bowl I saw Karl stroke into a monster. He made the drop and pulled himself up into a 20-foot barrel. It was a freight train ride that he would probably remember the rest of his life. Alec Cooke came out on a North Shore stiletto gun. It was the kind of day you really "picked" your wave. We were soon joined by Brain Keaulana. After my initial wipeout I had become gun shy. I guess when you get older other things become more important than stroking into a 20 foot wave. Cooke, Keaulana and Heyer were ripping. Ah...the reckless abandon of youth.

The waves were building and looking towards Kaena Point indicators signaled a set, as we scrambled for the horizon, the next wave loomed up and I spun around to take off. It looked sixty-forty against me making the wave. Years ago I probably would have been hyped up enough to stroke into the maelstrom, but I pulled back and ended up catching a smaller wave in. Yet, I still felt I belonged. The rhythm of the ocean was the same. Feeling the lineup, sensing the waves, time intervals, direction, position were still the subtleties of riding point surf at Makaha.

On the way back into town, I felt that an incredible amount of energy had been drained from me. I realized that the days of my youth were over.

Hemmings Shows Championship Form at Makaha
Fred Hemmings Jr. shows form that helped him win Makaha surfing championship yesterday. Details on Sports Page

Front page, The Honolulu Advertiser, December 23, 1966. The headline about the tragic war is historic.

The waves of Makaha still beckon me
for an occasional dance.

Sixties

We live our lives in the context of the time we are traveling through. Values change as society evolves. Are there basic moral values that should NOT change? Prior to the sixties, we lived in a sterile environment. Right was right and wrong definitely was wrong and had consequences. In retrospect, I feel the sixties were the pivotal years culturally and politically for America. Real change also escalated in science and technology. It is said that technology started to replace the industrial age in the sixties. History will record the sixties as profound for the American culture, curiously it was the same for surfing. In those 10 short years surfing went from being a relatively obscure pastime on the shores of Hawai'i, California, Australia and a few other locations to being an international sport and an economic force. Surfers had ridden long, wood boards for hundreds of years. By the end of the sixties, waves were being ridden on short, light boards made of foam. By the end of the sixties, America was riding a wave of change.

The Surf Report

We relied on calling friends for surf reports. There was little or no surf forecasting. The US Weather Bureau at the Honolulu International Airport could give sketchy information on North Pacific conditions. We depended on the telephone. On the North Shore, Val Valentine was the reliable source. At Makaha, we would call the Klausemeyers. They would always give an accurate report by looking out the front window of their house on the beach and reporting what they saw. Dependable reports were important. Before the highways were built, the commute to go surfing at Makaha or the North Shore was a long drive on a winding two-lane road. Buffalo was NOT a reliable source. He and his young family lived over the bathhouse at Makaha. When desperate, I would call him. Sometimes he would report: "Hey, Freddie, hurry out—the waves are terrific." I would rush out and find the surf terrible. Buffalo wanted someone to play with, so he would give me a bogus report, knowing I would race out to Makaha. We ended up having fun even if there were no waves.

One of my pals, Joe Tiepel, has built the current Surf News Network (SNN) here in Hawai'i. Surfers now get on the evening news a surf prediction for the next day and, in the morning, Joe's network provides accurate reports. The level of sophistication of surf reports and the technology involved are marvelous.

Val

Back in the sixties you would go to the North Shore and conveniently end up parking at a friend's house, using their hose to rinse off and sitting around after surfing for a bull session. Val Valentine was always a gracious host. The judges of the first couple of Duke contests sat on his porch. The early Duke contests were literally staged from the front porch of Val's home.

I don't think Val was ever a surfer. He was a surf photographer and produced 16mm films. In a little cottage shop business, Val made Paipo boards and wholesaled them to surf shops and friends. Paipo boards were plywood-thin belly boards that preceded the invention of boogie boards. There were a few hard-core Paipo surfers—let's see…John Wiedleich and Jim Growney are the two I remember. If you remember Paipo boards, you qualify as a vintage surfer.

Val and his wife were wonderful people. The little reef break on the shore fronting his old home honors his memory. It is called Val's Reef.

Duke Surf Team

Early in 1965 I was standing under the banyan tree at Kuhio Beach for a night surfing event. It was winter, so the swell on the south shore was not that great. The waves were junk, I wasn't surfing. A guy walked up to me and introduced himself as Kimo McVay. He owned the Duke Kahanamoku night club in the International Market Place and wanted me to be on the Duke Surf Team that he was organizing. The Duke Surf Team was going to promote Duke surfing products. I was 19 and did not have much business experience, so I asked Joey Cabell what he thought. Joey is older than I am and had been around the block a few times on business deals. Joey counseled me to take the opportunity if the pay was adequate and the business had potential for growth. Well, I ended up a charter member of the Duke Surf Team. The real compensation I would find out was the honor and pleasure of spending the twilight years of Duke's life with him. Money could not buy the experience. The original Duke team eventually consisted of Paul Strauch, Butch Van Artsdalen, Joey Cabell and myself. Joey was caught up in developing his restaurant, so usually Paul, Butch and I would end up going on the promotional trips. We always had fun.

Here I was, a young surfer, traveling with the modern-day *ali'i* of Hawai'i—Duke Kahanamoku and I shared those days with three of surfing's most dynamic men.

Butch, Paul and Joey...

Butch Van Artsdalen

Most of the people who knew him would agree that Butch was one of the most handsome and athletically gifted surfers in the sport. He looked like a dark-haired Robert Redford. Butch was drafted by a pro baseball farm team after high school. He could consistently punt a football 60 yards. He played basketball like a pro. This guy had it all. He also had a fatal flaw.

Someone should write the "Butch Van Artsdalen Story." Butch stories abound. He was the first Mr. Pipeline. A goofy foot, Butch perfected the art of pulling up tight into a Pipeline barrel. He was fearless. He rode big Waimea. Butch could switch stances naturally. He did it all. He also drank...too much.

Butch showed up in Hawai'i from San Diego and immediately endeared himself to the Hawaiian lifestyle. He became one of the boys on the North Shore. He was a lifeguard.

He also drank....

I can't remember why, but it is obvious whom Paul, Butch and the lovely young ladies are laughing at. We were at the CAVE bar in the Beverly Wilshire hotel during Don Ho's debut at the Coconut Grove. Kimo McVay gave us an open tab. We always took turns signing the bar tab. I always signed Butch's name. When he got his bill at check-out, I went into hiding, afraid that he would kick my butt. No matter. Kimo covered the costs of the entire trip, including Butch's horrendous bar tab. Don't worry, Butch got me back for my pranks.

We did have fun. Butch and I traveled with the Duke Team and ended up partying and being wild men together. I was a weekend warrior drinker, too. After bouts with drinking, Butch had one of the strangest habits ever. He would sleep in precarious places. We once dropped a young lady off after a date. I was driving my mother's old '56 Chevy wagon. We started to drive back home, and I decided it would be better to pull over and sleep it off. I awoke later to find Butch sleeping under the car. Once, in San Francisco, we rose in the morning after being out on the town to find Butch sleeping in a planter box one story up, outside a bay window. Everyone who surfed in the sixties has a Butch story.

This is sad. Butch was a terminal alcoholic. In the early seventies, when I focused my energies on the business of pro surfing, I dropped out of being a North Shore regular. Though great friends during our Duke Team days, Butch and I drifted apart. How tragic it was to periodically run into Butch and see that the ravages of alcoholism were slowly draining away his life. Butch drank himself to death at 38 years old. Alcoholism, like drug addiction, ultimately destroys lives. We gathered on the beach at Ehukai for his funeral. After eulogies by friends, we took his ashes out to the Pipeline lineup.

I learned too late that "enabling" a friend with a terrible chemical dependency like alcoholism is not what true friendship should really be. In Butch's case, we should have tried to help him stop drinking. God rest his soul.

Speaking of overindulgence in adult beverages, let me tell you this story:

Divine Intervention

In those days I also was a wild-man drinker. On occasion Butch and I dispensed much havoc together. The potential of a drinking problem existed for me, too. I would always stop drinking entirely before a major athletic event. In 1975, I began training for the Moloka'i-to-O'ahu canoe race. The Outrigger Canoe Club teams I paddled on won a few races in the sixties. Outrigger canoe paddling is a major sport for many of the surfers from Hawai'i. I stopped drinking completely on August 1, 1975 to get in top shape for the Moloka'i-to-O'ahu race in October. We won the race in an epic battle against an avant-garde team from Tahiti. I planned to go on a rip-roaring drinking binge to celebrate the hard-fought victory. It never happened. This is one of the stranger episodes in my life. I felt a deep and very powerful external force telling me not to drink anymore. Was this force the subconscious overcoming my conscious—was it my guardian angel?? Who knows? It was powerful. By the way, I know I have a guardian angel—otherwise, I would not have survived some of the wild adventures of my life. Without really ever consciously setting out to do so, I stopped drinking. It dramatically enhanced my life, as I could have ended up being a slave to alcohol. I did not drink for 17 years. In 1992, I started drinking a glass of wine occasionally with dinner. They say wine cuts fat and is healthy for you. I wish I could have divine intervention for my eating habits. I am thinking of going on the liposuction diet—lose 20 pounds in 20 minutes...just joking.

Paul Strauch

One of my best surfing buddies was Paul Strauch. He is on the list of Hawai'i's all-time greatest surfers. I used to call Paul the gentleman surfer. He had a fluid and smooth style of riding waves. His signature maneuver was to squat low on his board and stretch his left leg straight out in front of his body. That maneuver came to be known as the "Strauch stretch," also called a "cheater five." Paul did this on 12-foot waves at Sunset. Think about it—it's not easy to do on a big wave. When we were in Peru for the 1965 World Surfing Championships, Paul enthralled all the Peruvians with his suave style and gentlemanly manner. In fact, he really captivated one lovely Peruvian lady to the extent that she ended up in front of our hotel with her luggage on the day we were to return to Hawai'i. Must have been some miscommunication. Paul was one of Hawai'i's most successful competitive surfers. Of the amigos on the Duke Surf Team, Paul was the secret agent.

Paul was my best buddy. I was so thrilled when he won the 1969 Makaha International Championships. I always envied his suave surfing style.

Joey Cabell

Joey was, and is, a little older than the rest of us. He had already established himself as a successful businessman when the Duke Surf Team was formed. Joey and surfing pal Buzzy Bent of California were originators of the Chart House restaurants. Joey usually had other things keeping him busy and did not travel with us on the Duke Team promotional trips.

Joey, like Butch, was, and is, a natural athlete. He grew up surfing. Waikiki was his home and Queens was his play surf. Joey is a spick-and-span kind of guy. Everything is organized, orderly and under control. He seems to be focused always when surfing, knowing where he is and where he wants to go. He snow-skis as well as he surfs. The guy is still in ultimate shape. If you held a contest right now with all the best surfers from the sixties, Joey would be a top gun. Hey, that's a good idea—there should be a contest with the best surfers from the sixties. I think it should be at Makaha on a 15-foot day.

Joey Cabell—still in top shape.

Surfboards

All right, I might as well confess right now...I sometimes talk to my surfboards when revved up while surfing—one-way conversation, of course. I'll start to worry when I hear the boards talking back. When conversing with my surfboards, I say things like, "Come on, baby, we can do it," "Go fast," or "Whoa, take it easy." I keep the utterances simple. The boards usually responded well. As a result, most of my boards had names. Other surfers name their boards, too, so I did not feel like a weirdo being the only guy naming surfboards. I have since found out I am a weirdo for talking to my boards. Do you know anyone who has names for their surfboards? Most board names included the color. One year I had a white board and always wore white trunks. Never did wear black shorts…just kidding—relax, boys.

I would bet the all-time favorite name for surfboards has to be "Big Red," although my first board was **Big Orange**. When I was 8 years old in 1954, my dad finally purchased my first surfboard. Since we weren't well off financially, he acquired a vintage hollow for $10.

It was a monster. Anyway, he always worried when I went surfing, so he painted my natural brown hollow board international orange. I guess Dad figured if I got lost at sea while riding the wild waves of Baby Surf, I could be found easily. Big Orange didn't last very long. NO loss. I couldn't even carry it to the ocean by myself—it was too darn cumbersome.

My three favorite boards were:

The **Hornet**—a Yater special. It worked like magic, I could nose ride it real well. A curious thing happened. I banged up the nose of the Hornet real bad and had to replace the first 2 or 3 inches of the board. The repair job worked, but for some reason I lost confidence in the board. One's state of mind has a great influence on performance. After the "nose job," the performance of the Hornet had not changed much…just my confidence in it did. Sounds like cosmetic surgery. Think about it.

The Blue Max could tuck into a Makaha shore break barrel or drop into a 20-foot Waimea maelstrom.

The **Blue Max**—you should have seen the movie *The Blue Max*. It was about World War I biplanes carving up the sky in battle. My Blue Max carved up the waves and was my favorite for two winters. It was a semi-gun designed for waves from 6 to 15 feet. It was an incredibly versatile surfboard that could tuck into a 4-foot Makaha shore break barrel, or launch down the face of a Waimea monster. If I had to surf through life on only one surf board, I would choose the Blue Max.

Big Red—in the early sixties Dick Brewer was an icon of big wave surfboard building.

I was riding SURFBOARDS HAWAII and Dick told me that he had just made a "concave gun" for Buzzy Trent. I was intrigued and asked Dick to shape one for me. "**Big Red**," as the board was to be known, was designed to be a battleship. I wanted a board that was big and heavy, to handle giant and bumpy waves. In ancient Hawai'i, the *olo* board was a long, heavy board used in rough surf. Big Red was used as a modern-day *olo* board.

The winter of '64–'65 included some great days at Waimea. I had much confidence in Big Red. At close to 11 feet and weighing 48 pounds, once Big

Red gained momentum, it just kept rolling. In choppy surf Big Red was stable and could power through the worst of conditions. They are using the heavy board theory in "tow in" surfing now.

Big Red won Makaha. In 1964 the surf for the finals of the Makaha International Surfing Championships was 10-plus, barely breaking from the point. The finals were hotly contested, with nine competitors that included Strauch, Cabell, Keaulana, Downing, Cloutier, Harold Iggy, Rick Steere and Howard Chapleau. I was in contention to win and needed one more high-scoring ride. A set walled up outside. I spun Big Red around and took off on the largest wave. The notorious "bowl" loomed ahead, the percentages were against me to make it. I decided to go for it. The speed and momentum of Big Red carried me through the bowl for a high-scoring ride. That's how the board "Big Red" won the famous Makaha International Surfing Championships. *Surfer Magazine* recorded the ride in a sequence of photos.

The clairvoyants at *Surfer Magazine* had predicted my win in an issue **before** the contest. Those *Surfer Magazine* guys are so cosmic.

Surfboards Hawaii
1333 S. KING STREET
PHONE 503-087
HONOLULU, HAWAII

FRED HEMMINGS

In Over Our Heads With Johnny McMahon

Johnny McMahon was a Santa Monica surfer who came to Hawai'i and became a local boy. He rode big waves, was a major contributor to the Makaha International Surfing Championships, and was an all-around good guy. Though he was 30-plus years older than me, we were the best of friends. We often drove out to the North Shore together to surf. There were no surf reports in the early sixties, and we would take the long drive not knowing how big the waves were. So, on this one trip, we drove up to Laniakea late one afternoon. No one was out, and the waves appeared from shore to be 10 to 12. We hastily charged out. Well, when no one is surfing, it is hard to really estimate the size of waves, because there is nothing to relate them to. Most things in life have a perspective. It soon became obvious that the big sets were closer to 18 feet—considerably bigger than either of us wanted to ride alone that late in the after-noon. I took off on a smoker and kicked out down the line after a scary ride. A scary ride for me at the time was the type where you catch a big wave and pull up into it, crouch into a survival stance, and ride for your life. When I was paddling back out to the lineup, I saw Johnny take off on a monster. He got blasted. I was worried. I saw him come up and yelled and signaled him to the shore. I caught a reasonable wave and rode in. We decided that the surf was fantastic, but this late in the afternoon—it wasn't worth dying for. Were we a couple of wild and crazy guys? We laughed about the episode for years to come.

Surf with friends, good times are better when shared.

LSD

We experienced the start of the drug culture. Prior to the late sixties, you would occasionally read about "Bohemians smoking reefers" caught in a "drug den," or a report would appear in the paper about a heroin addict. Drugs were foreign to most Americans. It changed rapidly.

So, one day after surfing, we were sitting around Makaha Beach "talking story." This was in 1967, and the hallucinogenic drug LSD was coming into vogue. A prominent big wave rider at the time was a charter space pilot on LSD. He was talking on and on about the magic of LSD and how it freed up one's mind. He was almost lecturing us. Buffalo was not enthused. The guy kept going on and on. At one point the LSD guru said words to the effect, "You know, reality is what we perceive—like we could just be more imagining what

By 1969 the hallucinogenic acid trippers were ragging me because I was too regular—no trips for me. I had a surfboard ad run that stated my feelings about surfing. Notice my red, white and blue all-American board—there was a message there, too. I did get a six-pack of crappola for the ad from the hard-core space pilots. Such is life.

76

we are doing now." Well, Buff had enough. He calmly looked at our LSD friend and said, "How 'bout I punch your head? You goin' imagine dat?" Needless to say, our loquacious friend was snapped back to reality by Buffalo's wise and few well-chosen words.

Surfing Fashion

My pal Randy Rarick still hassles me because I don't dress like a surfer. I can get him really upset by wearing an ancient pair of Gucci loafers to the North Shore. There is a surfing look, and I guess Randy feels I am out of uniform.

A company named Lynn's provided custom trunks to the beachboys working at the Outrigger beach services back in the fifties. Soon many of the Waikiki surfers were wearing trunks made by Lynn's. I had a pair of light-blue Lynn's that I wore till they became "puka pants," which means they had holes in them. Takes and M. Nii evolved as custom surf trunk makers for the hardcore surfing crowd. Their trunks were the forerunners of board shorts. They made custom-fitted, colorful cotton trunks with drawstrings and stripes down the side. You just had to have trunks from Takes or M. Nii to be "in."

Smart surfing entrepreneurs in California saw the potential for creating surf wear as a manufacturing business rather than small-time custom work. Duke Boyd is credited with innovating the west coast look for surfing attire. Hang Ten, Surf Line, Lightning Bolt and other surf wear companies emerged and built a market. The California casual look in fashion repudiated the "uptight" fashion of the East. This was in tune with the whole LA/California mystique. Surf wear innovator Dave Rochlen says, "Surfing's biggest impact on fashion was to reject fashion." Surf attire is a huge international business now. surf wear has transcended surfing and become attire for young people around the world. Have you ever noticed that surfers, especially young surfers, are the biggest conformists around when it comes to how they dress? Fashion for surfers is almost a uniform. Check out the kids now with the baggy pants, T-shirts, caps on backwards—even sunglasses have to be the latest style. We went through several phases of fad attire in the sixties. For awhile, everyone was wearing sandals and even serapes from Mexico. The competition stripe was the thing for a season or two. Everything from boards and T-shirts to trunks had "competition" stripes.

I still don't dress like a surfer. I have always loved my aloha shirts. Jams World aloha shirts are classics. They are produced by Jams World founder and surfer, Dave Rochlen. Kahala Sportswear has been producing classic aloha shirts since I surfed with the Duke Team. In Hawai'i, surfboard companies Local Motion, Hawaiian Island Creations and Town and Country expanded into the clothing business. Fledgling companies such as Local 808 and North Shore Underground are emerging, as some bigger companies seem to grow out of their surfing roots and falter.

Surfing has an impact on fashion, and the surf wear industry was launched in the sixties.

The Locals

Riding the waves of Hawai'i attracted men and women from all walks of life. Here is the difficult part of writing about years gone by—I know I will inadvertently omit some luminaries of my time. Women of the waves featured the Sunn sisters, Sharon Weber, Bernie Ross and Joey Hamasaki. Friends who rode the waves included Ricky Steere, Gilbert Soyu, Brian Ho, Snooky Pai, Joey Gerard, Eric Parker, Wayne Miyata and Joe Kitchens. Surfing pals at Punahou School featured Buzzy Knuebuhl, Buzzy Lee, Jon Sutherland and Steve Paty. The list of Waikiki Surf Club, Hui Nalu and Outrigger Canoe Club buddies is long.

The Top Guns

Joining Joey, Paul and Butch on the sixties "top gun" list were Buffalo, Eddie and Clyde Aikau, Ben Aipa, George Downing, Kealoha Kaio, Bobby Cloutier, Barry Kanaiapuni, Tiger Espere and Billy Hamilton. Bobby Cloutier is an unheralded surfer from Hawai'i of the sixties. Look over the results of the big events—Bobby Cloutier was frequently in the finals. The next surge of super surfers featured Gerry Lopez, Jeff Hakman, Jimmy Blears, Rory Russell, Randy Rarick, Reno Abellira, Jackie Eberle and Jock Sutherland.

The Visitors

The surfers that dominated the scene in the sixties were classics.

Every winter Hawai'i hosted an entourage of wave riders from the major surf locations of the world. Surfers came to Hawai'i—the ultimate challenge.

The Greatest

Who was the best surfer from California? It was Ned Eckert, also known as JJ Moon. Ned Eckert was a hilarious guy who allegedly surfed. *Surfer Magazine* did a tongue-in-cheek interview with him, where he explained in detail why he was the best surfer ever. Many naive readers bought the story. Nobody laughed more than the illustrious Ned Eckert, a k a JJ Moon. Actually, the episode taught me a valuable lesson. You really didn't have to be a great surfer to gain fame. The magazines could do it for you. That is one of the reasons I was so anxious to start pro surfing and a circuit. Great surfers would be determined by performance in the water. Actually, many acknowledged Phil Edwards as California's greatest surfer in the early sixties. His graceful and classic style was envied and admired.

We enjoyed the yearly migration of California surfers to Hawai'i. The starting lineup from California featured Mike Doyle, Rusty Miller, Corky Carroll, Mike Hynson, Rich Chew, Mickey Dora, Mike Purpus, Robert August, Phil Edwards, Mickey Munoz, the young Rolf Arness, transplanted Hawaiian David Nuuhiwa and lady surfers Marge Calhoun, Linda Benson, Joyce Hoffman, Linda Nelson and Linda Merrill, to name a few.

Sorry, Corky

I had read something in a surfing magazine attributed to Corky Carroll that I interpreted to be a "dig" about Hawaiian surfers. I must have been having a bad hair day or in a down biorhythm cycle, because, when I ran into Corky at Paumalu, I verbally accosted and threatened him. It is close to 35 years late—Corky, I am sorry I hassled you.

Dana Point Mafia

A group of surfing trailblazers were called the Dana Point Mafia. I often wonder where the name came from. It is true that the majority of surfing's economic development in the sixties converged at Dana Point and its environs. The Dana Point cartel included Hobie Alter, surfing's most successful equipment manufacturer; Grubby Clarke, who started the foam blank business; Dick Metz, surf shop and merchandising wizard; Flippy and Walter Hoffman, textile manufacturers; Bruce Brown, whose movie *Endless Summer* helped promote surfing worldwide; John Severson, who created *Surfer Magazine*; and surfers Phil Edwards and Mickey Munoz. These surfers monopolized much of the economics of the sport and literally laid the foundations for surfing industries. They created product and controlled image and marketing. "Mafia" has other connotations; consequently, I think the name is a misnomer. The Dana Point guys are mostly WASP (White Anglo Saxon Protestant), not Italian. The Dana Point Cartel would be a more accurate name. As a group, they are entrepreneurs and successful—good for them. Their success is good for surfing, too.

Windansea Surf Club

In 1964 the Windansea Surf Club from San Diego showed up en masse for the Makaha contest—there must have been 50 of them. It seemed like every great surfer from California came to Hawai'i on the Windansea Surf Club team. They were led by Thor Svenson and stayed at a church pavilion in Waianae. I was made a member and given a pair of the team trunks.

That led to a little confusion when I experienced success in the competition. Somehow the word was spread that Fred Hemmings was surfing for Windansea Surf Club of California—OOPS. Fortunately, contest official Moku Froiseth pulled out

Even though they gave me a pair of Windansea trunks, everyone knew I always surfed for Hawai'i.

my entry blank that clearly stated that my affiliation was with Surfboards Hawaii, and the Hawai'i newspapers knew I was a born-and-bred local boy.

The East Coast

By the late sixties, surfing was flourishing in select beach towns on the East Coast. Surfers from Florida were starting to show up in Hawai'i. Cecil Lear was the leader in organizing East Coast Surfing. The trailblazers in the Hawaiian waves were Dick Catri, Bruce Valuzi and Gary Propper. A special award should go to Gary Propper, who arrived in Hawai'i and had probably never surfed a wave over 6 feet. Knowing his limitations, he slowly worked his way into the North Shore lineup and did well.

Peruvians

In March of 1964 I was invited to represent Hawai'i at the Peruvian International Championships. Punahou School gave me a pass, and I was off on a long journey to a strange land. Phil Edwards and Bo Beck represented California. Australian surfers were world traveler Peter Troy, Mike Hickey and Rex Banks. We were all guests of Club Waikiki, founded in 1941 by Peruvian surfing patriarch Carlos Dogney. It was my first exposure to a foreign culture.

The contest was held at Kon Tiki. It was the original and only frequented big wave spot in Peru. I noticed that the texture of the Peruvian waves was so different from Hawai'i. Waves do have "personalities." Some say that waves are like women. The waves in Hawai'i are sassy, powerful and arrogant. Kon Tiki, in Peru, provided waves that were slow, methodical and deceptive. The Kon Tiki wave did not look difficult, but looks can be deceiving. Most Peruvians at the time surfed right in front of Club Waikiki in Miraflores, on the coast of Lima.

Here are the Hawaiians and Peruvians at the 1965 World contest. (l to r, standing) Carlos Velarde, Fred Hemmings, Locho Miroquesada, Bobby Cloutier, Poncho Aramburu, Buffalo Keaulana, Miguel Plaza, Paul Strauch, with George Downing and Hector Velarde (squatting).

Surfing in Peru was in its infancy. The senior statesmen of the sport besides Carlos Doggy were Poncho Wiese and Edwardo Arena. Hector and Carlos Velarde, Miguel Plaza, Piti Block, the Barredda brothers, Poncho Aramburu, Rafael Navarro and the late Joquin Miroquesada made up the core of regulars.

The surfing ladies and gentlemen of Peru have a close and dear relationship with the surfers of Hawai'i.

The Shining Path....To Hell

For many years, from 1983 till about 1991, Peru was a dangerous country because of radical communists operating under the name of "sindero luminoso," or "shining path." When I visited the country in 1982, they were blowing things up and killing innocent people. The "shining path" terrorists closed the country for all practical purposes. The election of a tough president named Fujimura started the liberation of Peru. President Fujimura waged war against the communist terrorists and won. The country is now safe to travel to again. Just another reason why surfers should join me in fighting communism...just joking, again—lighten up. The reason I do bring this up is that there are magnificent surf sites in Peru and, I imagine, many more yet to be discovered. Peru should be a major stop on the ASP world pro tour. Peru has great waves, a colorful culture and, best of all, Peruvian surfers are full of aloha.

Peru, 1966, Como Se Dice?

Another fun trip with friends from Hawai'i. This happened in Peru. I am not going to name the famous Hawaiian surfer involved.

We were partying one day after a full day of surfing. Peruvian friends had country homes at Punta Hermosa, a town in the bay where the World contest was held the year before. One of my surfing pals, a big wave rider from Hawai'i, was making music and partying it up. A lovely young Peruvian lady was all over him and he was falling victim to her advances. She definitely was the aggressor. There was a very awkward communication problem, frustrating the blossoming relationship. The Hawaiian surfer could not speak Spanish and the lovely Peruvian lady could not speak a word of English. My Hawaiian friend became very frustrated. Realizing I spoke a little Spanish, he pleaded with me, "Freddie, tell this *wahine* I like give her the gas." It was obvious that he did not want to fill her auto with fuel. What he really wanted I could not muster the words for in Spanish.

The Surfers From Down Under

The surfers from Australia are very aggressive. I loved it because I was, too. This led to spirited competition and made my occasional victories over the Australians that much sweeter. Midget Farrelly and Nat Young are the Australian super surfers of the sixties. The Australian woman trailblazer in Hawai'i was Phyllis O'Donnell.

Russell Hughes, the enigmatic Peter Drouyn, Keith Paul and Bob McTavish were regulars in the international lineup. One winter, Bob McTavish made a big splash in the magazines. Actually, McTavish and his v-tail board also made some real big splashes spinning out at Sunset Beach.

The Mountain Men

Big wave riders are an elite group. They ride waves that can kill. Many people ask, "Why?" The answer is as old as humankind or as new as *Star Trek*...that is "to go where no one has gone before." Big wave surfing is a sport within a sport. The ingredients for success are guts, skill and luck. Big wave riders don't eat quiche. Big wave specialists would have been mountain men in the old west. I could just imagine them fighting bears, eating the raw meat of a fresh kill and living in the rugged mountains with nothing but their instincts for survival. The modern era of big wave riding at Waimea began in 1957, when Mickey Munoz, Mike Stang and a few other intrepid Californians ventured into the Waimea surf. The Hawaiian mountain men of surfing were stroking into the long walls of the Makaha surf. Big wave riders of the sixties were somewhat feral. The Waimea crew—Greg Noll, Ricky Grigg, Peter Cole, Jose Angel, Fred Van Dyke, Kimo Hollinger, Sammy Lee, Max Lim—were in a small fraternity. Makaha Point surf bred Wally Froiseth and Downing and several other Point surf aficionados. Curiously, Froiseth and Downing seldom, if ever, rode Waimea. They did not have to, because Downing and Froiseth owned Makaha.

The mountain men were "gun" bearers. Many of them did not even own boards for smaller waves.

Buzzy Trent retired from big wave surfing. He once explained to my pal Pat Bowlen and me why. Said Buzzy, "I was like a gunslinger in the old west. Every time Waimea was up, I was called out for a duel. The stakes would go up every year. I knew I would someday lose. I quit."

Latent Homosexual

Sports Illustrated did an article in 1965 about the "fringe" sport—surfing. Surfer Fred Van Dyke lit a firestorm of controversy when the article quoted him as saying that "most big wave riders are latent homosexuals." Hormone levels shot up in all the macho big wave riders when the article was read. The *Sports Illustrated* article was actually a hatchet job. It also misrepresented California woman ace Joyce Hoffman as saying, "California surfers are much better than Hawaiians because the Hawaiians are surfing for fun, not blood." That quote insulted both Hawaiian and California surfers. Joyce is a lovely person and I am sure her remarks were not intended to be ill-tempered. It was agreed by many surfers who read the article that the guy who wrote it was a twerp trying to create controversy rather than give an accurate representation of surfing. In spite of the article, no one that I know of ever questioned Fred Van Dyke's sexual preferences.

Endless Summer

I missed many photo ops while surfing in the sixties, though there are two situations that resulted in film and a photo still in use today.

In 1963 the famed Bruce Brown was paddling out with a water camera at Ala Moana. I was tired and catching a wave in. I sat on my board, turned, and was going to ride the wave sitting down. When spotting Bruce Brown pointing a camera at me, I stood up and turned 360 degrees, keeping my eyes on him as I surfed by. That was over 30 years ago. Now, kids who rent the *Endless Summer* video come up to me and say, "Hey, you're the guy sitting down in *Endless Summer*." Life can be cruel if you let it. All those years of surfing and I have been reduced to "the guy sitting down in *Endless Summer*."

Dr. Don James

If there is a Hall of Fame photographer in surfing, it has to be the late Don James. The Don James photos are now collectors items.

It was early in the morning of the Makaha Championships. The officials were announcing the start of the competition and wanted the water cleared. A few of us were sitting on the point. I ended up being the only guy out, trying to catch one last big ride. The announcer blared, "Fred Hemmings, come in right now or you will be disqualified." I quickly paddled down to the bowl to catch a wave in. A set jumped up and I took off. Dr. Don James was paddling out to photograph the competition. He sat up and took a picture. A mural of the photo was published and the caption read, in part, "bottom turn at the bowl." The mural is still in print.

The photo came about by accident.

The Swell of 1969

It was a week of 20-foot surf. We surfed Makaha every day. The North Shore was out of control.

Near the end of the week, the famous swell of 1969 peaked. It was one of those days that was bound to stay locked in the memories of everyone who experienced it. Early in the morning we all sat on the beach at Makaha, listening to the radio. The transmission was coming from the North Shore. This was the biggest surf to hit the Hawaiian Islands in recent history. The announcer was extremely excited, as he shouted out that another set loomed literally on the horizon. His estimate: the waves were 30, 40, maybe even 50 feet. From where the announcer was sitting on the bluff overlooking Waimea, the waves were breaking an easy mile out to sea. Those of us at Makaha were there because we knew that no one would get near the water on the North Shore. Surfing was out of the question. I remember how strange it was to listen to an excited voice on the radio screaming about mountains of water on the North Shore, and then about a minute or two later the "set" would thunder into the bay at Makaha. It was almost as if the man on the radio was a spotter for us at Makaha. The radio announcer would call the sets as they hit the North Shore and, sure enough, soon after the waves would roll into Makaha. A handful of us did surf that day. The surfers who paddled out included Charlie Galento, Rolf Arness, Jimmy Blears and Greg Noll. I was so scared, I was tempted to paddle to Pokai Bay to get in safely. It was a most memorable occasion, to say the least. They call it "extreme sports" now—that is the sport situation that can kill you. It was one of those surfing days that live vividly on in your mind.

Greg Noll took off on his famous wave later in the morning. I called it a death wish wave. He lived. Greg Noll has big…, lots of courage, and he was slightly crazed. Greg became one of my surfing heroes after that takeoff and surviving the wipeout. There is something to be admired in those who push the limits of human endeavors. Now, we joke that Greg is still riding that wave. It was a wave of a lifetime. That was Makaha, 1969.

The last year of the historical sixties spawned pro surfing.

It Was an Epic Decade

In the sixties, the years of my hard-core surfing, we were not pressed to seek out new and varied surf spots. Our surfing world was not crowded. In fact, when I started surfing, if you saw surfers go by in a car, you either knew them or you would try to find out who they were. In the years since then, I have had the occasion to surf many of the "newer" spots in Hawai'i and locations around the world. Though the future does portend many opportunities and adventures, I feel that the best time and place to be a surfer was the sixties in Hawai'i.

We had it all.

As I said—I dressed like an IBM salesman at the World contest banquet. Curiously, winning the World contest quenched my passion for surfing competition. I guess in some of life's pursuits, the journey can be more compelling than the destination.

World Contest

There were four World Surfing Championships in the sixties. I competed in two.

1965 World Contest

Peru hosted the 1965 World Surfing Championships. There was no professional surfing then, so the World contest was the ultimate competition. Getting to Peru was an exhausting journey. The Hawaiian team received a deal from Canadian Pacific Airlines. They would fly our boards to Lima for free. The catch was that we had to fly Canadian Pacific all the way, which meant flying Honolulu/Vancouver, BC/Calgary/Mexico City/Lima. Seems Canadian Pacific routes could not take us on a more direct journey. Buffalo and I saw snow for the first time in Calgary, Canada. Have you ever seen little boys playing in the snow? We indulged in adult beverages the first leg or two of the trip and were sick the rest of the way. I am still trying to figure out why we humans do things like that to ourselves. We survived and completed the journey to Peru.

In Miraflores on the coast of Lima, my roommates in the hotel cabana were Buffalo and Paul Strauch.

We gathered at the small Hotel Leuro before functions. The neatly attired group of surfers includes (l to r) Wayne Scheafer of California, Estelle and Joel DeRosnay of Biarritz, France, my mentor George Downing, Fred, Richard "Buffalo" Keaulana (I for some reason call "Buffalo" Richard), Wally Froiseth and Paul Strauch, all from Hawai'i. I can tell you we had more than our share of fun.

All the best surfers in the world were in Peru for the event. The contest was staged at a newly discovered peak on a point named Punta Rocas. The day of the finals, the surf was moderate in size, but rough. The waves were thick and broke in a bowl about a quarter mile off the point. The ocean was chilly, and we frequently had to dodge large jellyfish floating in the surf. The right lined up for a long ride and closed out in a relentless shore break. The lefts peeled off the point into the bay. Buffalo rode a beautiful wave all the way into the bay and almost out of the view of the judges.

I kept a journal of the trip. Here is the entry for February 20, 1965:

We awoke at 5:30 and caught taxis to Punta Rocas. No one was there till about 7:30, at about 9:00 they started the two semi final heats. Paul won the first heat with Mike Doyle, Nat Young and Felipe Pomar qualifying. I won the second heat with George Downing, Ken Adler and Mickey Munoz qualifying. We came in and rested for about a hour before they started the finals. The point was hot and crowded. I hadn't eaten a thing.

After the television people were finished the eight finalists were sent out. I rode Joey Cabells board at first because Paul was using my board, the one I used in the semis. I didn't want to use the gun because the waves were only about 10 feet. Maneuverability was going to play a prime factor in the contest. Joey's board was to light and after a few futile attempts to ride it I came back to the beach to change it for the gun. I spent the next 10 minutes trying to paddle out through the shore break., that almost broke me. In the water Felipe Pomar looked real good. Nat Young was getting hot small inside waves and Paul was performing on everything he caught. After a half hour a helicopter with a photographer onboard hovered over us and by the riders while on the waves. The 1 1/2 hours went by fast and the horn sounded. We came to the beach and eagerly waited for the results. It was fairly evident that Felipe was going to be victorious. This made me happy. If a Hawaiian couldn't win Felipe would surely be our choice. The results were:

8th	*Ken Adler, Australia*
7th	*George Downing, Hawai'i*
6th and 5th tied	
	Mike Doyle, California and myself, Hawai'i
4th	*Mickey Munoz, California*
3rd	*Paul Strauch, Hawai'i*
2nd	*Nat Young, Australia*
1st	*Felipe Pomar, Peru*

Mickey Munoz took off on the biggest wave. Really critical. The contest was well produced. So ended the world contest 1965.

We returned to the Club Waikiki for dinner. I had 2 steaks and six beers. got dressed and went to the hotel. The rest of the guys went to a television show. I stayed at the Leuro Bar with John Severson and Chuck Lennin. We went to Rincon Cafe at 8:00 for another steak dinner. (I guess I was very carnivorous then.) Then we came back to the hotel, I phoned Hawaii at about 9:30. We all went to Sunset Bar, the owner let us drink free. Buff turned on and got a guitar and cruised around the bar. I left early because I got tired of sitting on my ass. Came home at 1:00.

That is the entry from my journal. Seems like I ate too much steak and drank mucho cervasa. Buffalo made me do it…what a trip.

The 1968 World Contest

Selecting the team member for the World contest from Hawai'i resulted in some controversy. *Surfer Magazine* did an interview with me called "Hemmings is Hot." In the interview, I was outspoken and said what was on my mind. I have since learned some things are better left unsaid…for sure on that. I upset some in the Hawaiian Surfing Association by saying that I did not play the game of surfing in their local contests. My explicit remarks did not go unnoticed. The Hawaiian Surfing Association was the representative for the organization staging the World Championships. I surfed with a fair amount of success in the big international events but did not compete in the H.S.A. local events and, hence, I was not "rated." There were a few in the H.S.A who felt, as a result of not being rated, that I had not "qualified" to be on the Hawaiian team. Fortunately, an independent committee was formed to select the most well-rounded team possible.

I was honored to be selected.

I trained earnestly for the 1968 World contest. I did not indulge in alcohol, never did drugs. My mind was clear and focused. I ran and paddled every day to get in "top shape." Actually, I was the oddball. When in Puerto Rico for the championships, one of the contest directors, Rudy Huber, came up to me and asked if there was something "wrong" with me because I did not drink and party like the others. With a straight face, I said to him, "I will party after I win." He laughed. After the contest, he delivered a bottle of Chivas Regal to me so I could make good on my commitment. Rudy and I became great friends. Some of the surfing crowd, including a few in the surfing media, were caught up in the "cultism" of the time. Many of the surfers had a distinctive look. The uniform was Nehru jackets, psychedelic flowered shirts and beads. I wore aloha shirts, polo-style knits and jeans or shorts, and my hair was short. Even the speech of many surfers was novel, "Like, wow, man, heavy, get the vibes?" I spoke regular, with a smattering of pidgin terms. I pondered the blue smoke from thin cigarettes hovering around the heads of some. I joshed later..."I felt like an IBM salesman at a Cheech and Chong convention." I felt out of place with some of the surfers, because I was.

 I had to do well in the water because I could not control my surfing destiny on the land without compromising my values.

The contest waiting period dragged on for a week. Contest leaders Edwardo Arena and Rudy Huber were getting worried, having to postpone competition every day because of poor waves. The ABC crew was pressuring contest officials. They wanted to know where the waves were, not understanding that the venue for surfing—the ocean—was fickle.

At the end of the week, a swell finally arrived. The women's competition was hotly contested. The young and petite Margo Godfrey of California won over contest favorite and reigning first lady of surfing, Joyce Hoffman. Margo Godfrey Oberg married and came to Hawai'i. Her record as a competitor is unmatched.

To make a long story short, I ended up in the men's finals at Rincon Point. It was late in the afternoon. The waves were 6 feet, with bigger sets. The finalists were Russell Hughes, Midget Farrelly and Nat Young of Australia, Mike Doyle of California, Reno Abellira and myself from Hawai'i. I felt my assets were conditioning and strategy. I looked at the judges and asked myself, "What do these guys appreciate in surfing?"

I was not surfing for myself, I was surfing for the judges. My board, shaped by Ben Aipa, was a little longer and thicker than the popular style. It paddled well. My strategy was to go out, be patient and wait for the big sets. The lineup was a considerable distance from the shore, which worked in my favor. I surfed, carving long incisive lines, trying to climb and drop with a certain rhythm. My competitors' assets seemed to be the slash and tear technique of

I have never been a flashy surfer, but knew what the judges wanted. My Hawaiian style of surfing got the job done.

surfing, which was more difficult to appreciate from the distant shore. I would try to waltz with the waves; Midget, Nat and the gang were surfing "rock and rollers." Surfing was into rock and rolling, the judges weren't. The finals are still fixed in my mind. I was patient and caught few waves. Nat was consistent, just as he had been in events in Peru and at Makaha. He was catching many waves, but often missing the big sets. Nat was easy to beat. From what I could see in the water, the unpretentious Russell Hughes of Australia was doing real well. Midget was, as usual, strong. I caught what may have been the biggest wave of the finals and six other solid, bigger waves. Not many waves. Unlike years before at Makaha, quality—not quantity—was going to win.

While we waited on the beach for the results to be tabulated, I was quietly optimistic. The attention was focused on Midget. Supportive team members said it would be close and I was in contention. I'll always gratefully remember the moral support I received from Ben Aipa and Clyde Aikau. The wait for the results seemed to be forever. A tie had to be broken by going to the next wave. It was finally announced: Sixth Place—Reno Abellira, fifth—Mike Doyle, fourth—Nat Young, third—Russell Hughes, second—Midget Farrelly.

I had gained the honor of winning. I was proud to be a surfer. I was proud to be from Hawai'i. Midget was incredibly gracious. He is a world champion person.

Dick Graham

I understood I was not on the anointed list of favorites, probably because I did not conform to the pop culture of surfing. Though I was a rough, tough kind of guy, whispers by a few that Fred Hemmings should not have won did hurt my feelings. The unfounded doubts of my victory also made me mad. My record of success in major international competition was my evidence against the skeptics. I felt the doubts about my victory were based on the politics of surfing, not the facts or my record. I won fair and square.

Dick Graham, a surfing journalist, wrote the following. It was heartwarming for me to read it.

From
Surfing Yearbook
By Dick Graham, 1968

Standing proudly at the podium at the World Surfing Contest awards banquet Fred Hemmings looked briefly out at the audience, than at the table that seated the Hawaiian team. There was a slight hesitation, barely perceptible, that went unnoticed in the busy crowded room. The faintest hint of emotion. Then Hemmings stood tall, square shouldered and spoke clearly enunciating each word. "This is a very proud moment." In the next few brief sentences Fred accepted his title. There was much he did not say...much a champion feels that cannot be put into words, cannot be related in a busy crowded room. How does it feel to reach the pinnacle, the top, No. 1? What emotions race through a winner when he realizes that he is the victor in a hotly contested event.? Obviously there are many, all complex. Most of us will never know that moment. Unless his emotions betrayed him in that one glance at his teammates table. Hemmings was feeling a tremendous sense of elation, love and responsibility. Nothing like that can be adequately communicated in words, this complex web of intricate feelings. Coupled with the knowledge that once you are at the top you are the prime target. That those who did not agree with the judges decision will never forget the victory accorded you. Hemmings, in a dark suit and tie, clean cut, the image of the American athlete-had reached the top of surfing.

Dick Graham had read my soul and put it in words. It is the nicest thing ever written about me in the surfing media. Thank you, Dick.

As fate would have it, this was the last of the World championships that featured the best wave riding stars from each country. Pro surfing made its debut soon after, and most of the attention in the surfing world shifted to pro events. The World Championship became strictly an amateur competition. The surfing elite became pros.

The World amateur championships continue. It deserves more coverage and prestige. Contemporary pro heroes honed their competitive skills in the amateur events.

Where Glory Does Not Stay

Retiring Gracefully

I read a poem in high school by A.E. Housman about an athlete dying young.* The poem meant to me that a champion athlete dying young would always be a champion. I decided to quit competitive surfing soon after the World Championships in Puerto Rico. I was not planning on dying, but I figured all I could do is turn into an aging champion trying to hang on to the days of glory. ABC hired me as a commentator for coverage of the Duke, and I wanted to start a business owning and producing pro surfing events. So, I did.

If you get the chance, read the poem. It is bittersweet. There is a message for all the surf stars out there. Here is a verse from "To An Athlete Dying Young":

> Smart lad, to slip betimes away
>
> From fields where glory does not stay
>
> And early though the laurel grows
>
> It withers quicker than the rose

So many surfing champions of days gone by did not plan for the time when their laurels of glory would wither away.

Professionalism

The "Gunston" event in South Africa became one of the major pioneer events in pro surfing when it also offered a 500 rand (a little more than $500) purse in 1968. The 1969 Duke contest and the Smirnoff helped launch pro surfing. Soon after, in 1971, came the Pipeline Masters. Australia joined the movement later when the Bells Beach event turned pro in 1973. I am constantly amused by those who are trying to rewrite surfing history and skew the facts on what really happened.

"Fornicating With Mother Sea"

In the early years, just the concept of professionalism in surfing was controversial. One surfer said professionalism was "fornicating with mother sea..." Wow! I wrote an article for *Surfer Magazine* in 1969 to explain what I thought pro surfing would do to enhance the sport. I have to say it is never too late to learn something. I used the term "dope" in the article, because I thought it meant all mind-altering "illegal" substances. My daughters, Meaghan and Kaui, recently read the close-to-30 years old editorial and laughed. They explained to their naive father (that's me) that "dope" most often refers to marijuana. I certainly don't consider marijuana the plague that hard drugs are, especially if you are like President Bill Clinton and don't even inhale. Sorry, couldn't let that cheap shot slip by. I had not read the editorial for years. I was, and still am, an anti-drugs warrior.

Professionalism Is White
Surfer Magazine, 1969

(To this day, I have no idea what the magazine meant when it chose this title for my article—they had another article entitled "Professionalism is Black"—I guess the articles were used as commentaries on whether professionalism was "good" or "bad.")

Surfing needs professionalism! The most important job a professional organization would do is to qualify surfing as a legitimate sport. Amazingly enough, though surfing is a part of life for more than a million people in the United States alone, it is not truly recognized as a sport. Surfing seems to be in a limbo - neither here nor there. Some claim riding waves is an art, others say it is a cult or way of life...

Wait…this article is too long and *pedantic*—meaning lecturing in a patronizing manner. Anyway, I change my mind. I won't reprint the entire article. Let me summarize. At the time I felt pro surfing would:

1. define surfing as a legitimate sport.

2. help improve the image of surfing.

3. create a objective system of rating competitive surfers

4. provide the venue for advance surfing techniques

And I had my anti-drug crusade in the article.

I was very confident that the evolution of pro surfing would have a very positive impact on all of surfing.

What do you think? Has professionalism helped identify surfing as a sport, improved the image, promoted high-performance innovation and enhanced surfing economics for all involved???

Selling Surfing Events

Working behind the scenes with the Duke event, I gained an interest in the "business" of surfing competition. Selling a product that did not exist—pro surfing events—was a challenge. I figured that clothing companies, magazines and other surf-related businesses built a market—so could I. The difference was that pro surfing had to attract interests beyond the immediate surfing crowd. Our pal Joe Six Pack and his family living in Kansas needed to be entertained when watching coverage of surfing from Hawai'i. The other problem was to figure out how to make owning and producing surfing events fly economically. Surfing could not enjoy several of the revenue streams that other sports do. We could not charge admission to events on the beaches of Hawai'i. I had to rely on sponsorship and television rights fees. Many enterprising people have made a great deal of money in different aspects of surfing, including the clothing business and magazines. Creating profitable commerce of pro surfing would be a challenge—the first couple of years were lean for the surfers and contest entrepreneurs.

The Smirnoff

Greg Reynolds of the Heublein Company is an unrecognized figure in the evolution of pro surfing. I don't think he ever rode a surfboard, but, as a promotional whiz, he helped make professional surfing a reality. He decided that Heublein's popular vodka, Smirnoff, could get publicity by sponsoring a pro surfing event. Think about it—it was a long shot, at best. I know that corporate marketing departments get hundreds, if not thousands, of sponsorship proposals yearly. The fact that Smirnoff sponsored a surfing event is a wonder. The first Smirnoff was held in Santa Cruz, California, in 1969. Greg Reynolds brought the event to Hawai'i for better (and warmer?) surf. I was contracted to direct the Smirnoff Pro-Am. It was my desire to keep the event relatively small and mobile. Surfing events success is ultimately tied to the quality of the waves. All the hype and prize money in the world will not replace poor surf. The Smirnoff was made mobile to take advantage of the best surf possible within the waiting period. The first Smirnoff in Hawai'i was a challenge. We scouted Laniakea early in the morning. The swell was building, but the conditions were stormy on the North Shore. I called over to Momi Keaulana at Makaha. I asked her what she thought. Momi replied, "I'll beat the ocean with ti leaves. By the time you get here, the surf will be good." We caravanned to Makaha. The surf ended up 15 feet and excellent. Nat Young won $2,000. The Smirnoff people were ecstatic. We had pulled it off. The "mobile" concept turned out to be a success. In the years that followed, the Smirnoff competition was held at Haleiwa, Sunset, Laniakea and the '74 Waimea classic.

It ended as quickly as it began. Greg Reynolds informed me that the corporate marketing decision makers decided to drop the promotion. This was a valuable business lesson. Corporations sponsor events for marketing and community relations. Once an event no longer serves the purposes it was designed for, it is no longer valuable to the sponsor. Heublein had decided that sponsoring the Smirnoff contest in Hawai'i had run its course. The money spent on the Smirnoff surfing contest could be spent on a new promotion that would garner more "coverage." It may sound ruthless, but that is the way it is. I knew that for surfing to survive in a very competitive sports market we would have to build credibility and a broad audience.

Larry Lindberg and Professional Surfing

I tease Larry that he is the "grandfather" of pro surfing. Larry showed up in Hawai'i as an independent producer to cover the first Duke Classic for CBS in 1965. We became friends.

The first Duke contest was illustrious right from the start. All the surfers were guests at the Moana Surfrider Hotel in the heart of Waikiki and treated to wonderful hospitality.

On the first day of the waiting period for the competition, it was raining a typical December monsoon drenching. The surfing competition was postponed for the day. A few off us gathered in the lobby of the hotel to contemplate what to do. It was decided to go ti leaf sliding at one of my favorite "secret" spots in Nuʻuanu Valley. Ti leaf sliding is performed on a steep hill in a rain-slick muddy rut. I guess it is the Hawaiian form of a toboggan run in mud instead of snow and sitting on a ti leaf, rather than on a sleigh. Larry Lindberg joined us as we loaded up a truck to trek to Nuʻuanu. Wanting to ingratiate himself, Larry volunteered to buy some beer for the gang. We stopped at an adult beverage store in Moiliʻili and Larry ran in and bought a case of beer. Butch Van Artsdalen laughed and ran in and bought two more cases. We went ti leaf sliding. In spite of the Primo beer-induced bravado, we suffered no casualties. Larry Lindberg's first impression of surfers was that we were all kind of nuts. After watching us consume three cases of beer and ti leaf slide, we reinforced his assumption.

Larry Lindberg covered the World contest in 1968 for ABC Sports. He made it happen for surfing on TV.

In 1969, Larry convinced Kimo McVay, the promoter of the Duke event, to put up a $1,000 purse. Larry believed everyone, including television, surf magazines and clothing companies were making money from surfing and so should the surfers. We agreed with him.

Larry was extremely instrumental in garnering major television coverage of surfing and can be credited with spawning the growth of the sport on network television. Don't bother inviting Larry Lindberg to go ti leaf sliding—he won't go.

Network Television

The networks did not include surfing in their sports coverage because surfing was a big time sport. The reality was that in the early years, surfing was a novelty that had a strong visual appeal. Most, if not all, decisions in the business of sports broadcasting are economical. In the days before cable TV, the three networks dominated almost ALL the television market. They had the money to support anthology series such as *ABC Wide World of Sports, NBC Sports World* and *CBS Sports Spectacular*. It cost a heap of money to ship a TV crew to Hawaiʻi and put them up waiting for waves for a surf contest. I learned real quickly that surfing packages had to be appealing and economically competitive. A big factor in surfing coverage from Hawai'i was "snow." The networks covered the events in December but usually aired them in February or March. They wanted viewers in snowbound states to tune in to the warmth and beauty of Hawai'i. Andy Sidaris, of ABC, is a famous director who also covered college football. All directors have signature tactics in their coverage. You could always tell when Andy was directing a college game, because he would pan the stands for lovely ladies. Andy really enjoyed panning the crowd at the Hawaiian surfing events. Some believed that the scenery on the beach was as appealing as the surfing.

The economics of producing pro surfing competitions was a challenge. The "package" of contests was structured so the networks could amortize the costs coming to Hawai'i. It was tricky business.

Eventually ABC Sports cornered coverage of the Duke, Pipeline and Women's Masters. The World Cup was inaugurated for coverage by NBC. CBS accessed surfing with the World Team event. The networks were awash in money without competition from cable TV. They competed intensely. If one sports series had surfing, the others had to have surfing shows, too. We seized the opportunity and supplied the networks with events featuring the best surfing athletes competing for a prize purse in the ultimate waves.

Subjective Invitation, Objective Qualification

Believe it when I tell you that "selecting" participants for the Smirnoff, Pipe Masters and original pro events was difficult. With no rating system, the selection process was somewhat subjective. I never, ever wanted to be guilty of favoritism. My reputation and the credibility of the events were at stake. The problem remained—how to impartially select a field of competitors. We used as a foundation the results of major events such as the Makaha, Huntington Beach and Australian championships. After that, it would be more subjective. I consulted with individuals whose opinion I respected. A good friend, North Shore regular Bob Lundy, was always a help. He was never afraid to offer an informed opinion and justify it. Selecting a representative of emerging surfing countries to compete in the Hawai'i events created controversy. I tried to inoculate myself from discord by selecting the "country," not an individual, to be included in the event. An invitation would then be sent to the declared champion of that country or the selection would be made by the sanctioning surfing association of the country invited. This was done to promote interest in regions where the sport was new. It also helped to expand the pool of qualified athletes from the traditional powers of Hawai'i, California and Australia.

For instance, Doji Isaka from Japan was included in the first Smirnoff and that helped promote surfing in Japan, as well provide an international flavor for the event. I remember getting phone calls from an irate North Shore regular who read me the riot act because he was not invited to the Smirnoff. This "night bird" surfer was furious that he was not selected.

If you are a surfer, make believe you are going to invite six—only six—surfers to the Pipeline Masters. You cannot use ratings or results of prior Pipeline events. All you can use is your knowledge of "who" is hot at the Pipe. Try it, write the names down and then show them to a surfing pal. See if you get agreement.

The biggest help in the process of selecting a field of competitors was the inauguration of the "Pro Class Trials." This qualifying competition was the brainchild of Bernie Baker, Randy Rarick and Jack Shipley. It was a big relief to have an event that would narrow the field of contestants in an objective manner.

The Pipeline Masters

In 1971 we set up 10 folding chairs on the beach at the Pipeline and roped the section off with bunting for a judges area. The officials stand was a card table. Our public address system consisted of a hand-held bull horn. The prize purse added up to only $1,000. That was the first Pipeline Masters, over 25 years ago. The Pipeline Masters is now regarded as one of the supreme tests of professional surfing skills. Ironically, in the beginning there were a few who said that having a contest at the Pipeline was too dangerous. It is dangerous, but that is what competition at the highest levels is all about.

The Masters was originally conceived to be an event for just the surfers who could handle the Pipeline. The six competitors in the first contest were Mike Armstrong, Jock Sutherland, Jimmy Blears, Jackie Dunn, Jeff Hakman and Corky Carroll.

We surveyed the surf every morning to decide if the event was on. After several days, the surf looked promising and we put the decision on hold. Gerry Lopez, an invited contestant, asked Corky Carroll if the event was on. Corky said, "No." The event got underway several hours later. Gerry Lopez missed it. That is the Lopez version of the story—Corky's may be slightly different.

The surf was 6 feet. Jeff Hakman, surfing backside, won the first Pipeline Masters.

I put on a suit, went to New York, and convinced ABC Sports to cover the Pipeline Masters. John Bernards, boss of Offshore Sports Wear, was the big sponsor during the formative years. That started my career of "packaging" events for network television.

Here is how ABC coverage was lost, or at least how I perceived it at the time. One season we waited days for the surf and nothing happened. I was starting to panic because the ABC crew from New York was restless. They could not understand why there were no waves. Trust me when I say the worst part of producing surfing events is waiting for waves. We worked so hard to produce quality competitions, but controlling the waves was not in our domain. Running an event is especially difficult in Hawai'i because the standards are so high. Many contests around the world would be conducted in 3-foot shore break. In Hawai'i everyone expected 8- to 10-foot waves, or better.

I met Randy and Bernie Baker in the pitch dark every morning on the beach. We would strain our eyes, hoping to spy or even hear a wave. Of course, Randy and Bernie would be in contact with every surf seer around, although surf prediction was not a perfected art. ABC was upset, the media was balking, and I was under great pressure to get the event underway. This one morning Randy and Bernie said a swell was coming...tomorrow. The surf was 2 to 3 feet. I watched it for an hour and a 4-foot set came in. I panicked. "Randy! Bernie! Dead ahead, the surf will be great this afternoon when we send the finals out." They begged me to hold off till the next day. "Nope! I'm the big boss and paying for all this. The event is on." ABC set up and we started the event. That afternoon the waves were 1-1/2 to 3 feet for the finals. ABC was not happy. The next day the waves were 10 feet and perfect. All these years later, I can still hear Randy and Bernie laughing. Actually, ABC dropped the coverage of all surfing, including the Duke event, because of costs and the emergence of cable television.

Hawai'i's Derek Ho displays a cool style at the 1985 Pipeline Masters. It is hard to be cool on a wave that can slam you to death on the jagged coral reef.

Tom Carroll wears the helmet of victory at the 1982 Pipeline Masters.

The list of winners of the Pipeline Masters includes Gerry Lopez, Rory Russell, Shaun Tomson, Larry Blair, Jeff Crawford, Mark Richards, Simon Anderson, Dane Kealoha, Joey Burrand, Tom Carroll, Michael and Derek Ho, Sunny Garcia and Kelly Slater. Sounds like the Hall of Fame.

It is amazing how diverse perceptions of surfing can be. We sometimes perceive what we want and feel. I stood on the shore at the first Pipeline and, in the ensuing years, watched intently all the competitions.

I would marvel at the incredible tube rides of the Masters, but the most awesome wave in my memory was Martin Potter's excursion on a 12-foot wall of moving ocean in 1976. The wave was so clean, so overwhelming, so magnificent. Martin Potter seemed to glide to the bottom of the wave as it thundered behind him. The hush of the crowd intensified the moment. The curl chased him like a predator running down a helpless prey. The silence of the spectators turned to a cry of anticipation—would he escape? It was a surreal wave that punctuated all that the Pipeline is.

Martin Potter riding the beautiful beast.

Bring Back the World Team Championship

The truth is—unless you are a hard-core surfer, watching one surfer competing per wave can get redundant. I always thought the World Team contest was my most innovative production.

In A.S.P.-sanctioned events, an interference rule is strictly enforced—one surfer to a wave. The World Team event was created to promote interference. Here is how it works. There are two surfers on a national team who surf against two others on the other team. There is no interference rule. For safety reasons, the only limitation is "no contact." The surfers could drop in, fade back and stuff the opposition. Go-behinds, cutbacks and stalls are useful tactics. One team member could act as a blocker, while the other could be the scorer. Strategies would be up to the imagination of the combatants…I mean, competitors. At the end of the heat the highest scoring five waves for the team would be tallied to determine the winner. The World Team Championships was covered by CBS for several years. It was exciting and could be again. How about Hawai'i's Sunny Garcia and Derek Ho going head-to-head with the Florida team of Kelly Slater and Todd Holland at Haleiwa on a 10-foot day?

International Professional Surfing

In 1968, when I wrote the "Surfing Needs Professionalism" article, it seemed like a good idea to rate the world's top pros in an internationally sanctioned circuit of events. We had to wait till 1976—till there were enough events to originate the circuit. Behind-the-scenes leaders in the early stages of pro surfing included Peter Burness of South Africa, Bill Bolman of Australia and Kevin Seiter of California. We decided to recognize the events for the first rating year after the events were held. Some balked at it, but not Peter Townend, who was declared the first International Professional Surfing Champion. He won nothing but the title and he has been using it well since— good for him! I would like to think that the honor and prestige of winning helped the pros build their careers.

Randy Rarick and I ran IPS at a deficit. Randy received a small stipend to cover expenses.

Randy Rarick, Bernie Baker and Jack Shipley were key people in the formative years. Judging contests was very subjective and quite controversial. Jack Shipley evolved the system to success. Jack deserves much credit for working quietly behind the scenes and creating the foundation for the very sophisticated judging system.

International Professional Surfing was incorporated in Hawai'i as a non-profit organization. This was done specifically for the reason that I felt the circuit should be run as a cooperative effort between the surfers and contest owners. The surfers would profit from the prize money, endorsements, etc., and the contest owners and producers would profit from producing quality events. I did not want to interject another money-making entity into the mix. I was in a potential conflict-of-interest position, being owner of events and operating the circuit with Randy. We formed a board of directors to set policy. Peter Burness of South Africa was like a breath of fresh air at the annual meetings. He managed to be the broker for compromise between divergent interests. Kevin Seiter, originally from California, a young attorney/surfer, helped keep IPS meetings semi-coherent. The annual IPS meetings were something to behold. I don't think the U.S. Congress could make things more complicated. The meetings would drive me up the wall. My goal was to have IPS be the catalyst for marketing the sport in order to gain more sponsorship and coverage for individual surfers and events. I felt the time, energy and money consumed by the IPS bureaucracy could be better spent on the individual events. It was also important to make sure the sanctioning organization did not conflict with events and surfers' individual sponsors. The growth rate of total prize money from a modest start was good. In 1983, I was confronted with the takeover by the Association of Surfing Professionals...OK.

Association of Surfing Professionals

When we started International Professional Surfing here in Hawai'i, we did not consider IPS a money-making enterprise. I was in the business of owning and operating events and Randy Rarick was the director. We knew that a sanctioned circuit of pro events would benefit all concerned. There seemed to be too much pushing and tugging at the IPS meetings. Surfing politics and economics played a role at the long, drawn-out sessions. Surfers were seeking to build a more sophisticated management organization. In the meantime, Ian Cairns was "competing" against IPS with a separate circuit. Cairns gained the financial support of the Ocean Pacific company. It appeared that, with the lure of Ocean Pacific's money and the desire of the surfers to control the circuit, change was inevitable. Randy and I were spending money, time and enduring too much contention in the administration of IPS. Randy, sensing opposition to my tenure as "czar," bailed out early. Randy called me "czar." Pretty good metaphor, except he never called Ian Cairns a "Bolshevik." The wish of the surfers to change management of the world pro tour in 1983 was not resisted. The circuit had rapidly outgrown my desire to guide it.

The Association of Surfing Professionals took over the supervision of the circuit of contests. I was initially concerned that there could be a sponsorship-and-TV-rights conflict between individual events and the ambitious A.S.P. leaders. This feeling was reinforced by my previous experience with Cairns and Co. trying to subvert my events. I still feel that there exists a delicate balance between those making a living from A.S.P. and those who own and operate surfing events. As it has worked out, A.S.P. has done an adequate job maintaining the balance and managing the circuit. Under the current leadership of Graham Stapleberg and others, A.S.P. is poised to leap into bigger and better business opportunities.

The Triple Crown

This was a no-brainer. We produced three prime events on the circuit. The marketing value of linking them together made sense promotionally and economically. The tactic was very successful with horse racing. I copied it.

Women of the Waves

The first woman pro surfer was Laura Blears. Greg Reynolds of Smirnoff asked if a woman would compete in the Smirnoff. After an interesting discussion, it was decided to invite a woman to compete with the men. Talk about equal opportunity.

Laura was absolutely terrific. She paddled out into her preliminary heat at Laniakea. The waves were 6 to 8 feet. There is no affirmative action in the surf and male surfers are not known for chivalry. Laura did well in her heat, just missing qualifying for the next round. The door to women's pro surfing had been opened.

It is difficult for me to comment on the current lineup of women pro surfers, since I have been out of the business for a number of years. I can comment on the women who pioneered pro surfing. They were the best. Margo, Lynn Boyer, Rell Sunn, Sherie Gross, Jericho Poppler, Linda Scott, Debbie Beecham made women's pro surfing a reality. It was not easy. Just by the sheer numbers, women are at a disadvantage in surfing. What do you think? Do men outnumber women 10 to 1? In the early days of pro surfing, it was even more lopsided. The number, or lack of number, of women surfers impacts the sport. In the talent pool—if the total number of women surfers is small, it stands to reason the number of superstars may be proportionally limited. The economics of pro surfing were affected by the limited number of women. The women's surf business was almost nonexistent. It is changing. In the early days of pro surfing, the marketing was geared toward the men. It was difficult to get sponsorship for women's pro surfing. Though the ever-lovely Jericho Poppler would argue with me otherwise, the lack of big money sponsorship was an economic problem, not gender bias. The pioneer women worked hard to improve the quality of their performance. It was my desire to push the women athletes to the limits to improve the level of the excitement of the competition. The women pro surfers rose to the challenge. We waited for better waves, sometimes having the competitions in 10-foot surf at Paumalu, or the turbulent waves at Haleiwa. They did it and surfed exceptionally.

Classy ladies—Margo Oberg, Lynne Boyer, Jericho Poppler, Linda Scott, Debbie Beecham, Betty Depeolito— were pioneers of women's pro surfing in the early seventies.

JUST DO IT !!!!

Attention: Lisa Anderson, Layne Beachley, Rochelle Ballard, Emmanulle Joly, Keala Kennelly, Megan Abubo and women surfers of the nineties.

I cannot think of any reason why women should not be riding big surf. Many women surfers are as strong and durable as some of the men riding big waves. Women are physically capable to ride Waimea. Why not? I haven't figured it out yet. I think Margo, Lynn, Jericho, Debbie and the first women pros rode bigger waves 20 years ago than those the women are competing in today. Maybe that is because we tried to conduct women's competitions in bigger waves. I ran into Lynn Boyer the other evening at Kailua Beach. I asked her why women are not riding bigger surf after all these years. The question seemed to perplex her as much as it does me. In developing women's pro contests, I realized that women's surfing had to make it economically and could not rely on advancing on the coattails of the men. The marketplace of pro sports is a great equalizer. Prize money is based on performance and the resulting economics of the marketplace. Trust me when I tell you that the corporate prize money given to men is not a testosterone-based decision. In order for women's pro surfing to grow, the athletes are going to have to expand their capabilities, and events should generate more revenue. Women's basketball and volleyball are making great strides because women athletes are performing and audience attendance is up.

Here are my recommendations to women pro surfers:

1. Develop a strategy, schedule, get a coach and train to ride big waves.

2. Ride big Paumalu, Makaha and get into the lineup at Waimea.

3. Get big wave mentors.

4. Work with contest organizers to produce women's events in bigger surf.

5. Hold the women's Masters at the Pipeline.

6. Originate a women's event to be held only when the surf is "big."

Don't rely on men to make it happen. JUST DO IT (no swoosh intended).

The Pro Surfer

According to the news stories, Sunny Garcia is making over a quarter million dollars a year as a pro surfer. His career earnings is approaching $500,000. Kelly Slater is rumored to be making $1,000,000 with endorsement contracts. Top pro surfers are making serious money. They have worked hard. The smart pro surfers can parlay their assets into long-term financial security. Pro surfing has, excuse the cliché again, "come a long way." The quality of performance in the water is incredible. Kelly, Sunny, Barton Lynch, Derek Ho and entourage are executing maneuvers that could not even be imagined 20 years ago. They train hard. This is significant. Today's pro surfers are very well-tuned athletes. Many cross-train in exercises that increase cardiovascular condition, muscle strength and endurance. They are aware of how important nutrition is to performance. Surfing's best are high-tech athletes. The "international" field of participants has expanded to include surfers from Tahiti, Brazil, France, Japan and numerous other nations, as well as the powers of Hawai'i, the USA continent and Australia.

For all-around talent, I would stack up surfing's pros against the top athletes in any other sport. Pro surfers have the agility of gymnasts, the conditioning of distance runners, the aquatic skills of Olympic swimmers and the courage of bullfighters.

The Sports Industry

Sports is a big industry in Hawai'i. I claim that Hawai'i is the water sports capital of the world. Hawai'i is the venue for the best surfing, windsurfing and world-class sailing. Dennis Conner trained in Hawai'i before he went to Australia to win back the America's Cup. The North Shore is the mecca of the surfing world. Paia on Maui is the windsurfing capital of the world. The Ironman Triathlon was created in Hawai'i—great story. The International Billfish Tournament in Kona is the world's premier billfishing event. Hawai'i canoe and kayak teams are gaining Olympic recognition. Hawaiian outrigger canoe racing is becoming an international sport.

As a legislator and a surfer, I always wanted to have civic officials recognize, nourish and develop Hawai'i's surfing and water sports resources. Though I am not in the legislature anymore, I have not abandoned my quest to get amenities like bathrooms and park facilities at Paumalu and Makaha.

We can be proud that surfing has done so much as a source of pleasure, a sport, an industry and to exalt Hawai'i. This letter was intended to emphasize that surfing events on the North Shore are a huge asset to the State of Hawai'i. The letter to the editor appeared in a Honolulu newspaper in 1981.

HAWAII IS THE WINNER WITH THE HAWAIIAN PRO TOUR OF SURFING

At a time when we are worried about a leveling off in the state's largest industry, tourism, International Professional Surfing has given us some more good news.

It will sanction the Hawaiian Pro Tour of Surfing (Offshore Masters Classics, Op World Cup competitions and World team Challenge) again in 1981. These events, all on Oahu's fabled North Shore, have been featured on the American television networks for years. The competitions generate international coverage in all media.

The Hawaiian Pro Tour of Surfing events are aired on television at a time when much of the mainland is enduring record cold temperatures. Through out the winter season SEVEN separate surfing events are featured on network television. The TV shots of our lovely people and visitors enjoying the surfing events on our beautiful North Shore do look pretty enticing.

The promotion and international exposure that go along with Hawaiian Pro Tour of Surfing are a real boost for the Hawaii travel industry.

Letter to the editor —Fred Hemmings
2/3/81

Emulation

Big-time surfers are role models to many young surfers. I wrote this somewhat rambling article about the responsibility. I think the top surfers have to put forth the best image possible.

International Surfing Magazine
published 1970, edited 1996

Maybe, lurking at an obscure little break somewhere in the wave world, is a young person who will someday be a surfing superstar. There are, needless to say, many factors that will ply and mold a surfer into a reputation. The most influential single factor in the transition from obscurity to stardom is the individual. The positive attributes of the surfing elite are many. Basically, a physical coordination is needed, but the physical is vastly overshadowed by desire and by devotion to the cause which is to become the most in-tune wave rider possible. Many psychological reasons can motivate a surfer to becoming a superstar. Ego, recognition, identity, fame and fortune may all contribute.

As a surfer gains the physical prowess necessary to be recognized as a superstar, the media becomes important. Unfortunately media distortion often builds a stronger case for or against the surfer than really exists. Through this process comes the magic image of the surfing superstar. The image is sometimes a mirage. The surfing superstar must be a positive influence not only for the surfing community but more importantly for everyone who comes in con-

tact with the sport. It is fine that the elite in surfing know what is happening but herein lies a matter of concern. The surfing super stars have a heavy debt and responsibility to the wonderful sport of surfing. With them they carry the representation of the great surfing life. The surfing elite must feel an obligation to their fellow surfers to present the best on behalf of our sport. The gift of surfing has brought the super stars much. They in turn must represent the sport with as much dignity and honor as possible.

In 1988 I sold my proprietary interests in the individual events and the Triple Crown. Close to 20 years of the surf event business and a desire to focus on my political career led me to sell.

I am proud of pro surfing.

As a young surfer in 1968, I had the honor of presenting the exquisite World Championship perpetual trophy to the late John Burns, Governor of Hawai'i. I never suspected I would surf into politics.

Surfing Politics

The Locals vs. the Bronzed Aussies

In the early days of pro surfing, Ian Cairns and Peter Townend decided to "market" themselves as a team in the business of pro surfing. It would put me in a difficult position. I understood what they were trying to do and, frankly, felt surfing could use a few provocative characters. The "Bronzed Aussies" surely fit the bill. Cairns and Townend showed up for the surf season in Hawai'i in jumpsuits and with an aggressive "style" that did not endear them to the North Shore regulars. An articulate surfer referred to them as the "bronzed anal ports," also known to many of the locals as the "bronzed ass holes." On one occasion I literally had to intervene to keep them from getting punched out.

After winding down the "Bronzed Aussies" initiative, they turned their attention to creating a "circuit" of pro competitions and producing their own events. Hmmmm. I got infuriated when Townend and Cairns even communicated to ABC Sports that my events were renegade competitions. They created a lot of grief for my business and then showed up on the North Shore as if nothing happened. ABC Sports understood that they were competitive opportunists trying to replace me. Over the long run, it has all worked out. In the short run, they made business difficult. I would have been more than happy to help them with their pro surfing business...in Australia.

Ian is now successfully running a circuit of events, mainly in California. He won the 1976 World Cup competition. Years later, during the World Cup in 10-foot surf at Haleiwa, Ian and I had a grudge surf-off during the intermission. Ian, the word is: I kicked your fanny. I just might consider a rematch if you think you could handle it. Peter Townend is a very successful surf entrepreneur and has a beautiful family in California.

Get a Chuckle at This...
"Transnational Corporate Imperialism"

It is such a great line, "transnational corporate imperialism," that I have to tell you how it came to be. One year at the Pipeline contest, the ABC television producer came up to me and inquired why an Australian film crew using surfer Cheyne Horan as a commentator was filming the contest. I went up to them and asked and was promptly informed that they were covering the event for Australian television. We welcomed "news" coverage, but worldwide event telecast rights were bought and paid for by ABC Sports. There is a big difference between a minute's worth of news coverage and a half-hour show for sponsorship. I informed the Australian producer that ABC owned the telecast rights and infringing on them would jeopardize the event. The Australian basically told me to stuff it. I was caught between ABC Sports, who was paying to help make the event happen, and a most obnoxious Australian film crew that was attempting to pilfer coverage for sale in their own country. The ABC producer was upset. So, I did all I could do—I informed Cheyne Horan that, since he was getting paid and participating in the pirating of ABC rights and thus jeopardizing the event, I would have to suspend him from the next competition. The Australians were furious. They came to me and said they would use the footage only for "news" purposes. They lied. Several months after the event, an Australian surfing magazine came out with a version of the episode and accused me of "TRANSNATIONAL CORPORATE IMPERIAL- ISM" because I threatened to expel Cheyne from the event. After reading the Australian article, I couldn't figure out if I had made the "big time" by being guilty of some international crime, or if the author of the article suffered from some sort of down under paranoia. I still laugh every time I remember the line.

The Black Shorts

It was a big financial risk and much hard work to build the business of pro surfing events. As with many lucrative ventures, those who did not contribute in the lean years want to get on the gravy train when and if it starts to roll. In the early days of the competitions, clearing the water and maintaining safety was easily accomplished. As the events grew and became more numerous, everything became more complicated, including water safety. Bob Lundy suggested I hire a fledgling group on the North Shore that was starting a "lifeguard" business. The group I would find out later was a local *hui,* or club, that eventually would be called the Black Shorts. California transplant surfer Eddie Rothman seemed to be one of the leaders of the group. I can't remember exactly how this came about, but I ended up with an appointment to meet with Black Shorts representatives at the Kuilima hotel to negotiate a lifeguard contract. Randy Rarick conveniently could not make it. I took his aid, Beth Martin. We walked into the lobby of the hotel. One of the representatives of the group we were to negotiate with looked fearsome. It appeared like they hired him from central casting in an attempt to intimidate me. Beth Martin was visibly scared. We sat down. The demand was that I pay $7,000 a day for "security." My mind was a clenched fist of anger. I forced a smile on my face as I walked out. It was apparent what was happening. I went to every law enforcement agency in Hawai'i, explaining the situation. They all said they could not do anything till "something happened." How reassuring!! I could not wait till "something happened." Several days later, I received an anonymous call warning me not to talk to the cops anymore. Obviously the police had a leak. I could not rely on law enforcement agencies for help. The problem could have spelt the end of the events. No other group or lifeguards wanted to compete for the business. They understood the predicament, also. After laborious negotiations, a compromise was worked out and the events continued on. Many in the surfing world, including the surf magazine publishers, have complained to me about the fear and intimidation being perpetrated by a handful of North Shore regulars. Ironically, the magazine people who complained the loudest would then feature the "terrorist" individuals they were complaining about. Talk about hypocrisy. I have to emphasize that the overwhelming majority of Black Shorts members are good guys. I always said they would look better in white shorts.

Getting Blind Sided, a k a False Cracked

I literally had to take licks to save an event I was producing. For a few years, along with the surfing competitions, I packaged a Jet Ski race. The course was set through the surf at the Kuilima Hotel (Turtle Bay now), and the competitors were selected by the Jet Ski sanctioning organization. I created wild card positions for the North Shore Jet Ski experts. Actually, because the North Shore competitors knew how to maneuver in surf, they were serious contenders against the touring Jet Ski pros. One of the North Shore competitors was Brian Surrat, whom I had known for years. After his heat in which he did not qualify, he became enraged and, for some reason, wanted to take it out on somebody. I think Brian felt somehow he had been robbed by the results that left him out. I was the event owner and knew that excessive controversy, much less a fight with officials or TV personnel, would probably kill the event and even dampen NBC's desire to come to Hawai'i for all the competitions on the North Shore. I interceded. Brian hauled off and false cracked me. It was a good shot. My instinct was to punch it out right there. Cooler heads prevailed, Brian backed off, and I had a sore jaw. NBC honchos heard about it later.

Producing events for TV was not always as glamorous as some would believe.

Not So Righteous Man

My long-standing opposition to drugs sometimes put me at odds with the surfing underground. When I was elected to the Hawai'i Legislature, I cut back on my surfing activities. In the meantime, I was proud to be honored as an Association of Surfing Professionals "life" member. In that capacity and feeling that the sport of surfing should make a strong statement against drugs, I called on A.S.P. to institute a drug-testing program as was being done in pro football and the Olympics. I learned in the Legislature to never take a hard stand on an issue until all your "homework" had been done. I knew that drug testing had stood the test of constitutional law. A prominent surfer from years gone by took out a newspaper advertisement denouncing my initiative and ridiculing me. The thrust of the ad was the "constitutionality" of drug testing, a subject I am sure my adversary had not studied up on. The costly anti-Fred Hemmings ad was in a major Honolulu newspaper. I guess it was intended to embarrass me politically.

I cannot think of anyone who has benefited from a drug habit, though there are a few surfing punks who have made big bucks from selling drugs, often at the expense of young surfers and Hawaiian kids on the North Shore. I can think of too many surfers who wiped out their careers and lives because of hard drug consumption—some have died. To their credit, the Association of Surfing Professionals ended up taking a stand in favor of drug testing. It sent a strong message out that surfing would join other responsible sports in fighting drug abuse.

The Bad Boy Sell

The character and personality of surfing has been influenced (tainted) by what I call the "bad boy sell." Down through the years, a few surfers and commercial interests have used anti-establishment-in-your face marketing to sell their products. The "bad boy sell," which highlights punk imagery, has impacted surfing.

In my day, there was a surfer who was hot at Malibu—how can you not be? Here in Hawai'i, he was just another surfer. It turned out this guy was a small-time con man and ripped off people regularly. He became a surf cult hero. It always amazes me that some surfers give the finger to the "establishment" and then complain that the establishment does not go out of its way to help surfing. Too bad. Fortunately, all the positive and healthy aspects of surfing have overshadowed the "bad boy" marketing. Thanks, again, Duke, and all the surfers who bring dignity to the sport.

The Surf Media

The surfing media covers the Hawai'i events extensively. Hawai'i is where the action is. I understand that public opinion, and especially surfer's opinion, is influenced by what is written in the surfing magazines. I also understand that editorial coverage and reporting are sometimes influenced by advertising revenues. I did NOT advertise my pro surfing events in the magazines. I always rationalized that I was not selling pro competition to the surfers, so I did not need to advertise in the surf magazines like a clothing company does. I'll advertise this book in the magazines.

I must say that most of the coverage of the Hawai'i pro events is provocative and interesting. Some coverage gets caught up in the politics of the sport and could reflect the agenda of the editor, the writer covering the event, or big advertisers. During the years I owned and produced the Triple Crown events, I would read the coverage in great detail. My favorite surf journalists included Phil Jarratt and Drew Kampion. Phil Jarratt, of Australia, was never shy about letting his opinion interfere with the facts. I did not know if he was pulling everyone's chain or really believed everything he wrote. Drew Kampion also wrote incredibly amusing and hazy renditions of the Hawaiian scene. Amazingly, there are editors and writers who, to this day, consider pro surfing some sort of commercial sellout even though they are profiting from the sport. When I felt facts were being sacrificed at the altar of adversary journalism, I responded. It was fun jousting with some in the surf media. They would have the last word. You remember the saying, "Never argue with someone who buys ink by the barrel"?

Long Board Media

The surfing media is diversifying with the growth of the sport. Long board surfing is being "rediscovered." The coming of age of the baby boomer generation of surfers has created a more mature surf market. The long board surf media has emerged as a growing force in surfing and is defining a new segment of the surfing economy. In the United States the *Longboard Magazine* targets this growing and mature market. Longboard magazines are being published around the world now. Check the magazines out. The "old" guys will stroke back into the limelight. Keep alert for long boarders. We are back in vogue and are *coming down, sliding right* and taking no prisoners.

Keep the Country, Country

The north shore of the island of O'ahu is special and must be a sanctuary from excessive development. There are places that should be preserved.

Hype

In politics they warn about the politician who "talks the talk, but does not walk the walk." Look past the hype and look at the record—actions speak louder than words. We live in a very "marketable" society. Surfing reputations are often built for commercial purposes. When a large company needs to promote a product, it often hires a surfer for publicity, and the magazines go along with the hype because of advertising revenues. In the recent past, reputations were built for certain individuals and then, when they showed up in Hawai'i, they would be "on the shoulder," not even in the lineup. Image makers in the media would often select characters that fit their agenda.

Actually, surfing competition helped put the focus on performance rather than hype. Look back on the recent history of surfing and recall the surf stars whose reputations were celluloid and magazine-generated that have not stood the test of time. Hype is an interesting phenomenon that permeates all aspects of our society.

Surf the way you feel, not the way others may dictate. "Be true to thyself." — Shakespeare surf team

Surfing politics...well...is a pain in the ass.
I'd rather be chasing waves.

The Legends

Surfing is rich with legends and distinctive characters. In giving thought to writing about legends, it occurred to me that the "test of time" is important in gauging contributions in almost any field of endeavor. Which deeds in the history of surfing have stood the test of time? Which surfers' achievements, both in and out of the ocean, have endured and have had a positive impact on others? In addition to Duke Kahanamoku, some choices in Hawai'i from my perspective are:

George Freeth

"He is a brown Mercury, his heels are winged and in them is the swiftness of the sea." Jack London's words, as legend has it, were inspired by a Hawaiian athlete named George Freeth. He is credited with introducing surfing in Southern California.

Freeth, born in Honolulu in 1883, was invited to California in 1907. Freeth put on a display of surfing that astounded all who came to Redondo Beach to see him. A commemorative bust of George Freeth honors his memory at Redondo Beach.

George Freeth is also credited with promoting water polo and lifeguarding. At the youthful age of 35, George Freeth died. He inspired the young and young at heart in California to take up the sport of his ancestors—surfing.

Legend Buffalo Keaulana greets the world while his trusty steersman guides him to shore.

119

Tom Blake

When you read about Tom Blake and his long life of magnificent exploits, you realize what an innovative genius he was. It is also apparent that Tom Blake loved and respected the Hawai'i of yesterday. His book *Hawaiian Surfboard*, published in 1935, preserves the legends and folklore of ancient Hawaiian surfing. It seems evident Tom Blake was also a man of great passion who lamented the erosion of the Hawaiian culture as the Islands evolved into the twentieth century. Tom Blake was from strange shores but gained the respect of the surfers of Hawai'i and became a son of the waves of Waikiki. His development of the hollow surfboard was an innovation that took surfers off solid wood boards of close to a hundred pounds and allowed them to shoot across the waves on his sleek innovation.

"The man with a Hawaiian heart."

I am including this article my buddy, the fabled Tommy Holmes and I wrote to substantiate the genius of Tom Blake. He was the da Vinci of surfing.

Surfboard Sailing
co-authored by Tommy Holmes and Fred Hemmings, 1988

Over the years Hawaii's wet and wild womb has given birth to some spectacular water sports, board surfing being the best known. Less well known is that surfboard sailing also had its genesis in Hawaii, brainchild of Tom Blake, a pioneer, visionary, superb waterman and consummate gentleman.

Wally Froiseth, surfer and canoeist, remembers some 50 years ago sitting out at Castles, a large deep water break off Waikiki, hearing Tom Blake tell him about his plans to build a "sailing surfboard."

In his younger days, Blake's mind apparently churned as much as the waves he so loved to surf. Blake, now in his 80's, was the first to develop the hollow surfboard, a vast improvement over the very heavy solid boards then in use. "The first one appeared in 1929...it was 1934 before a really good model of that construction was perfected."

Within months of the debut of the hollow surfboard Blake contrived, after experimenting with different mounting methods, a sail rig for his board - seen in the accompanying photographs.

In a 1935 treatise entitled Surfboard Technique, Blake included a section called "Sailing the Surfboard." In it he comments that "many different success-ful sailing rigs have been tried on the hollow surfboard. It can be rigged like a canoe, steering with the feet." He goes on to note that "the best of all and the least trouble is to sail before the wind by lying prone upon the board and using a large beach umbrella as a sail. If the wind is from offshore, paddle out a half mile or so with the umbrella, sit upright upon the board when opening, then sail back to shore."

For the more serious surfboard sailor he says a "standard canoe mast is lashed to the board. Sideboards may be used, also a rudder, but they are not necessary. The sailing surfboard can be steered with the feet."

In 1932 Blake intuitively wrote that "the future will see surfboards....throughout the world..." But he was always one to give credit its due, noting "and so it may be plainly seen that the Hawaiians have given the world an idea (the surfboard) that while once nearly obsolete to the world, has been rescued from the lost arts and encouraged by Duke and his beach boys, now promises well to give health and pleasure to the youth of the world."

While surfing is indeed the Hawaiians' gift to the world of sports, it was none other than Tom Blake, a man years ahead of his time, who gave the world the first "sailing surfboard."

Eddie Aikau

I wrote this for *Surfing Classic*, a publication in Japan, after Eddie was lost at sea.

A Personal Tribute to Eddie Aikau
Surfing Classic Magazine • Japan, 1978

I can remember those days at Waimea. The atmosphere seemed to be charged with the awesome energy of the breaking waves. The North shore would be under a shroud of salt water mist. Those were the days Eddie, that I guess very few people in the world of surfing can even begin to understand. Sometimes we would spend what seemed to be hours just watching, seeing what the huge surf was doing. Paddling out was always time to do some deep thinking, as a matador must do before facing a charging bull. I can remember those special days at Waimea were your days. In the lineup at Waimea sitting, waiting, you were the master. You would always seem to be in a impossible position on take off. It seemed like you had a special ticket that allowed you to catch the huge Waimea waves so deep in the line up, an area where no one else would venture. Those were the days, Eddie, the feelings, the exhilaration, being scared, panting for a breathe powering into waves, free falling, skipping across

121

the face of a mountain of moving water. It is hard to communicate those feelings.

I can remember the surfing contests, the parties, getting together at your family's house and talking story. The family, Eddie, always the family, the Aikau family seems to be so much more powerful than any one individual.

Then this winter, it started out to be a winter just like the rest, big surf, the pro contests and everything else that makes up the North Shore lifestyle during the surf season. Eddie, there was something different with you. I can see your face. It was like destiny had seized your spirit and was taking you. I can remember the Duke contest. You knew you were going to win. You brought pride and honor to your family, to your Hawaii.

We were friends who rode the waves – Eddie and I saunter down the beach to compete in the Duke Classic.

Then Hokulea, many people just don't understand that the Hokulea is more than the duplication of an ancient Hawaiian craft. Sailing with the Hokulea was the hopes of the Hawaiian people, seeking to regain pieces of their disappearing culture. I can remember, Eddie, how consumed you were in this effort. Destiny continued to pull you.

Eddie, when the Hokulea swamped soon after setting sail for Tahiti, I knew your action was instinctive, your years of rescue work, your superb knowledge of the ocean made you the one to paddle for help.

FATE, Eddie, your path was destined. You paddled into eternity. The legend of Eddie Aikau, Keiki o ka nalu, "child of the waves." ALOHA, Eddie.

One of surfing's most clever events is the Eddie Aikau Memorial event put on by Quicksilver. The event has existed for many years, but only two or three actual competitions have been held. Those Quicksilver guys are very cunning. They get a tremendous amount of publicity and rarely have to pay prize money or produce the actual event. I must say that, when the contest has been produced, it has been epic. It would be great if it was held every year, but then, again, it probably gets more notoriety by not being held. It is a great event that pays tribute to Eddie Aikau, Keiki O Ka Nalu.

Eddie is remembered and honored in the surfing world.

Wally Froiseth

Wally Froiseth, who is a man of great stature in the sport of surfing, has been obscured by more flamboyant stars. Wally is a pioneer in the water. He and his cohorts at Makaha wrote the book on riding point surf. Can you imagine taking off on 15- to 20-foot waves on skegless solid wood boards? Wally won the Makaha Championships. Wally **was** the Makaha Championships. He represents all the **best** the sport of surfing is.

Wally is so respected that he was automatically made the head judge of the first Duke Classic in 1965. Sitting on the porch of Val's house put Wally and the judges on the 50-yard line of Paumalu.

There are leaders in the sport who have given much back. Wally Froiseth and his wife, Moku, were prime moving forces in the success of the Makaha Championships.

The Froiseths and friends from the Waikiki Surf Club made the Makaha Championships the first of the truly world-class surfing events.

Waikiki Surf Club has been a powerhouse in the other great Hawaiian sport of outrigger canoe racing. In the last several years, teams from Waikiki Surf Club have been winning races in a koa racing canoe made by Wally. Wally worked generously to help the famous Hawaiian voyaging canoe, the *Hokulea*, sail into modern Hawaiian history.

Every great Hawaiian surfer who honed his or her competitive skills at the Makaha contest owes Wally a debt of gratitude.

Wally Froiseth is a Hall of Fame surfer. He has given much to the traditional Hawaiian sports of surfing and outrigger canoe racing.

Rabbit Kekai

Check the record—no one has surfed and won more contests than Rabbit Kekai. That is because Rabbit started surfing in the late 1920's and loves competition. Rabbit won at Makaha. Rabbit won in Peru. Rabbit wins age group divisions in events around the world. He is over 75 years old and surfs like a kid.

"That's nothing" is my favorite Rabbit Kekai line. We all love Rabbit, and one of his most enjoyable traits is his vivid imagination. No matter what you are talking about, Rabbit can come up with a "that's nothing" one-upmanship.

Some of his "that's nothing" stories are accurate, as opposed to folklore.

Rabbit is truly a man of the ocean. Like the patriarch of modern surfing, Duke Kahanamoku, Rabbit has spent his life in the ocean and waves of his Hawai'i.

Carlos Dogny

Carlos Dogny was the ambassador of surfing in South America. He introduced surfing to his native Peru in 1941. After visiting the Outrigger Canoe Club in Hawai'i, Carlos returned to Peru and founded Club Waikiki in Miraflores, on the coast of Lima. Peruvian surfers recognize Carlos as the founding father of surfing in their country. Carlos traveled the world and frequently surfed at exotic locations. Pioneers of surfing in Biarritz, France, remember Carlos warmly. Carlos was in Biarritz from

Carlos Dogny was a gentleman of fine taste who spent his life surfing the waves of the world.

the earliest days of surfing in France. Carlos never married, although it is said that many women around the world enjoyed his charm. Surfing was his perpetual mistress.

CONTEMPORARY HEROES

This is completely subjective, and many will challenge my opinions. I am writing about individuals who symbolize something larger than themselves. I am writing about people, events and times that helped mold the personality of surfing.

From my perspective, contemporary heroes include these classics:

The Keaulanas — *a surfing family of Hawai'i*

Buffalo is not an ethnic warrior fighting politically correct battles. He is doing a better job of preserving his heritage by being a Hawaiian living his culture. This editorial was published in the *Honolulu Star-Bulletin* in 1980, soon after Buffalo's big board contest.

Ancient Hawaii at Makaha

published February 29,1980

Honolulu Star-Bulletin

The morning was ominous. Thick gray clouds hung over the ocean. Up on the hill overlooking Makaha Beach the Hawaiians made ready. As it happens yearly, the beach had eroded, but this year even more so. The modern restroom was falling into the sea. The black rocks of the old railway retaining wall stretched a hundred yards along the edge of the ocean. Those who know were undisturbed. They realize that yearly mother nature takes the sand of Makaha to clean it and that the gentle swells of summer would return the beach.

At the Keana Point side of Makaha a throng of people had gathered. They stood amidst a stage, tower and concession booths. The parking lot was filling quickly as more people arrived.

The crowd was mixed. A few tourists, some town locals, but mostly Hawaiians. The sound of conch shells reverberated off the side of the valley. The same conch shells that are used in the staged tourist shows that go on in jet age Hawaii, but these conch shells heralded a different note...old Hawaii. There clear solid sound brought echoes of hundreds of years ago. The crowd hushed. The atmosphere suddenly became charged with the electricity of human emotion. The emotion of the Hawaiians. the emotion of their nation, culture and way of life.

The emotion of pride and the emotion of their very existence seemed to grip the all present.

Then down the hill came the heralds, stopping to blow the conch shells and fill the air with timeless sound. Everyone knew ancient Hawaii would follow. In royal procession they came. First the warriors, young, strong, muscular warriors in gourd helmets carrying wooden spears. These are the warriors of Makaha. The real warriors. They were tense, almost in a trance. Eyes glistened with the tears of held back emotions.

The kahuna, the priest, the elder, wise sage with his elite entourage followed. Vestiges of the royal and sacred party were held aloft. The kahuna's chant was lucid, slow and deliberate. His message was not some idle chant of a bygone era. His chant was in his native tongue, but the message was clear. "All present, prepare and take heed. From the hill overlooking our Makaha beach comes history, comes the Hawaiians.

More warriors carrying a platform on which sat Ka Moi the king. The silence of the crowd was gripping. The men carrying the platform seemed to strain, not from the weight of Ka Moi, but strained from the sheer drama of these moments.

Ka Moi, the king. Buffalo Kalolookalani Keaulana. A face of a thousand years. A face drained by the rigors of modern life, a face made rugged by the burden of leadership, a proud face, a face of a warrior king, a determined face.. yet a face of compassion. A face that reflects the glory and dignity of his people. A face that all looked up to.

Directly behind Ka Moi came young men whose destiny would have them take up the heritage of the king. Men whose young lives shadowed the Ka Moi. Their heads were held high. Their presence was strong yet yielding to the Ka Moi

On the next platform came the Ka Moi wahine the queen. A Kaahumanu returned. A woman that all did respect. A mother to a nation. The queen, French Desoto for those few moments seem to embrace her people to her bosom, bringing security and warmth as only a mother could. Young ladies followed, quiet ladies of noble appearance, warriors closed the procession.

The entourage took positions on the stage. There was chanting, song and special words of a keiki o ka nalu.

The ceremony was reverently dedicated to a lost brother, Eddie Aikau, now a legend. The Aikau family bravely looked to the sea. Ka Moi stood, warriors cleared the way to the shore. Out to the sea on surfboards with attendants Ka Moi paddled with an offering, a hookupu to the god of the ocean.

They turned, caught a wave, up to the beach they rode, hand in hand. The crowd screamed and cheered. The spell was broken. The games, music and fun were to begin.

Momi

There are times when circumstances in life demonstrate who your true friends are. My son, Heath, was on the Waianae coast surfing with friends. On the highway back to town he passed a car, and his car tire hit a rock on the road that flipped up and hit the other car. The occupant pursued them. He was crazed and chasing after the kids with a vengeance. Heath drove up Nanakuli Valley to Buffalo's house. The kids entered the driveway with the wild guy in pursuit. Heath and his friends jumped out of the car and ran to the Keaulanas' porch. The irate driver got out of his car with a gun. Momi, Buffalo's wife, stepped out of the house and stepped between the children and the menacing man with the gun. She screamed at him words to the effect that he is making a big mistake and better leave. The man backed down. She put herself in harm's way for my child.

Momi Keaulana is a strong woman and has done much to bond the dynamic Keaulana family.

This is a reprint of an old newspaper ad for the original Jams. Design wizard Dave Rochlen arranged for Paul Strauch, George Downing, Fred Hemmings and Buffalo to model his new creation.

Goodyear Turkey

Sometimes when the surf was not good at Makaha, we would find other things to do. One year, on a surfless day, Buffalo and I decided to go hunting. Armed with .22 rifles, we walked up Makaha Valley through the *kiawe* and bushes. Like great hunters (which we were not), we stalked dangerous wild turkeys in the harsh terrain of the Serengeti…I mean, Makaha valley. To our surprise, we actually found and bagged a big turkey. The turkey was so lame we probably could have thrown a stone and nailed it. We suspected that the turkey may have been from the Chinn Ho land. I was not too anxious to get arrested for turkey rustling at Makaha. Curiously, Buffalo picked up the turkey and offered to pack it back. Great, I figured I could run faster if we got caught.

We came to the clearing several hundred yards before the highway. Buffalo threw the turkey on the ground, announcing that it was my turn to "haul" the turkey. That shrewd Buffalo carried the turkey through the cover of the bushes and, now that we were in the clearing and near cop country, it was my turn. Buffalo is resourceful. Momi cooked the turkey. It was like rubber. We called it the Goodyear turkey.

I don't have the time to tell you all my Buffalo stories. Let's see—there is "The rat patrol," "Watermelons in Peru," "The Chinese restaurant eyes story," "drinking pisco (it is a Peruvian liquor and tastes like it sounds)," "poking fish"—heck, I can't even write down the titles of all the Buffalo stories—maybe in the next book. P.S. You'll love the Rat Patrol story—public service at its best.

THE HAWAIIANS

Kealoha, Kaluiokalani, Kanaiapuni, Puu, Aipa, Kalepa, Kalama, Keaulana, Aikau — *to name a few*

They are protectors of the realm. They have preserved the surfing legacy that has been passed on to them. Dane Kealoha is power. The smile on the face of Buttons Kauiokalani reveals the merriment of his character. Diligence is the hallmark of Kanaiapuni. Mel Puu, a son of Makaha, reflects the versatility of his surf. Ben Aipa is the coach. Archie Kalepa is a Hawaiian waterman in canoes and on the waves. David Kalama challenges the jaws of killer waves. The Keaulanas are the first family of surfing. The legend of the Aikaus endures. These are some of the names that are synonymous with surfing in Hawai'i. They have greatly enriched the sport .

Rell Sunn — *the Queen of Makaha*

It was the finals of the Tandem Surfing Championships at Makaha. Rell and I were hired to do the "expert" commentating for *ABC Wide World of Sports*. The director came up to Rell and me and described exactly how he wanted to open the show. Here it is... "You and Rell go out into the surf, catch a wave, and ride in tandem, with Rell on your shoulders. When you hit the beach, put Rell down and run up to the boom mike and talk into the camera, welcoming everyone to the event...got it?" Obviously the director had not the

When we rode in together on this wave for the ABC cameras, Rell was the boss. The kid on the body board is Rusty Keaulana, now a world champion long board surfer.

faintest idea of how difficult the timing and surfing would be. Rell and I paddled out on a huge tandem board. It was our first time tandem surfing together. In the lineup we caught a gentle wave. Rell stood up, grabbed my wrists and hopped onto my shoulders. She rode regally, all the while "directing" me to shore (actually, I am being nice). She told me what do in very explicit terms for the entire wave. We rode up the beach on the back of the wave, stepped off the board and sauntered up to the camera and microphone. I still marvel that we did it just as the naive TV director had outlined. She made it happen by the sheer force of her will and my knowing that if I did not perform as she dictated, she would give me scoldings. The "sheer force of her will" means Rell is a human of tremendous spiritual strength.

She radiates.

Menehune

Look at the faces of the children coming out of the water after competing in Rell Sunn's Menehune Contest. Their little faces say it all—the joy of surfing. Here are a few things Rell has given back to surfing. Rell created and has produced the Menehune contest for over 20 years. Many of Hawai'i's top pros experienced their first taste of competition in the Menehune contest—ask Sunny Garcia.

She is an accomplished and stylish surfer. Rell was a pioneer woman pro surfer. I distinctly remember that Rell, along with the ever-lovely Jericho Poppler, was the most outspoken and strongest advocate for the women of the waves. Rell Sunn is the matriarch of surfing in Hawai'i.

Aunty Rell took a horde of Menehune surfers to the Biarritz surf festival. Trust me—even with the help of accompanying mothers, it was an arduous journey. I forgot that small kids always are in high gear. Rell managed. The Menehune were great ambassadors for Hawai'i.

130

Randy Rarick

When we were in Tokyo, he knew his way around. In Paris and Biarritz, he led the tour. When we were in Australia together—you guessed it—he showed me around. He has surfed waves on remote African coasts, the exotic Pacific Islands, South American frontiers and Indian Ocean retreats. Randy Rarick is surfing's international man. Wherever he goes, he is recognized and welcomed

He has actually traveled to over 100 countries and, where there are waves, he has ridden them. Randy's home on the North Shore is like a United Nations depot.

Once when we were in Tokyo together, we searched for a "real" Japanese restaurant for lunch. After a long walk far from the hotel, we found a charming, and what appeared to be modest, place to dine. We ordered by pointing at the menus, as neither of us could communicate adequately in Japanese. I'll never forget the lunch. The waiter brought out dish after dish of exotic food. Each morsel was gift wrapped and arranged on the plate most elegantly. I felt guilty eating the arrangement. It was like we were eating an art show. The price of our authentic Japanese lunch was equally as stunning as the food. We had a pot of rice at the end of the meal to top off the tanks.

Many wave riders do not know Randy surfed in the first Hawaiian Smirnoff. In the early years of pro surfing, Randy was a competitor. It wasn't till 1974 that he started to work with the Hawaiian Pro Tour by directing the events I produced. He is the best. We worked together well. I was constantly in high gear and running over anything that got in the way. Randy is circumspect.

Margo Oberg — _the First Lady of Surfing_

She was a 15-year-old girl in Puerto Rico when she won the World surfing championship. She was destined to become the most successful woman surfer in the sport. Margo Oberg's résumé of victories reigns supreme in women's surfing. Never has one athlete so dominated women's pro surfing. Margo won the ABC Women's Masters and World Cup events several times. Some of the women pro events in the mid-seventies were held in 10-foot-plus surf on the North Shore. Margo was in the lineup and taking off on the big sets. She dominated in California, Australia and even Brazil. Has any woman matched her record since? What is most interesting— I bet if a contemporary women's event was held at Paumalu in 10-foot surf, Margo would be a contender.

Margo Olberg and I enjoyed the awards banquet at the World surfing championships in 1968. The picture now appears as though we were both attempting to get on someone's best dressed list. Surf attire has changed since then.

131

Mike Doyle — *the Athlete*

Mike Doyle would have to be nominated as one of California's all-time surfing athletes. In every contest final I was in, there was Mike Doyle. He rode small and big waves. This was significant to us in Hawai'i. Many surfers gained reputations that were tamed by Hawai'i's big surf. Mike Doyle rode big waves. Mike Doyle was a triumphant competitor who did well in Hawaiian events.

Winning a competition in California's 3-foot surf is far different from winning in 10- to 12-foot surf at Paumalu. Mike Doyle won in both venues. Mike Doyle was a premier tandem surfer. His wife tells me he still is a great tandem surfer. He raced paddle boards and is an all-around waterman. Mike Doyle is one of California's greatest surfers—ever.

Duke and I congratulate Mike Doyle for being the Surfer Poll winner in 1964. It pisses me off—Doyle STILL looks the same. He hasn't aged.

Midget

Midget Farrelly is Australian. He captures the essence of his homeland. Midget is bold, competitive and proud. Midget is a man of substance and sincerity. Midget surfed vigorously and surfed to win. He forged new paths in world surfing for the Australians. The legions of impressive Australian surfers to follow would carry on the standards set by Midget in the sixties.

Ricky Grigg — *Surfing's Scholar*

He missed the first Duke Classic because he was earning his doctorate in oceanography at Scripps Institution of Oceanography in La Jolla, California. He returned to Hawai'i and won the next Duke contest. Ricky is a premier example of a "waterman." He was one of America's original aquanauts. He is a leading expert on coral reef ecology and a world-renowned oceanographer. I respect Ricky because of his integrity. For example, there is a controversy on the North Shore regarding the development of a large subdivision called Lihi Lani on the hill overlooking Pupukea. We all want to keep the country, country. It is true that the development would change the character of the North Shore. However, many of the militant opponents fabricated environmental reasons concerning waste water disposal as a foundation of opposition. It would be very easy to get on that bandwagon, but their position has no basis of fact. Interestingly, the biggest source of ocean pollution on the North Shore are the cesspools of beachfront homes owned by many of the very people who are the most vocal critics against the development. According to scientific studies, the near-shore bacteria count in the ocean area of these cesspool homes is highest. Ricky has the integrity to stick to the facts, rather than get on the politically correct bandwagon.

The Best Pro Surfer

Tough call. I am bias toward the Hawaiians, but I have to stay true to my belief that, in competitive surfing, performance in the water is what counts. My experience and **the record** lead me to believe the best "pro surfer" of the formative years was Mark Richards. It is no coincidence that he is a true gentleman and worthy representative of our sport. Tom Curren and Kelly Slater are on my list for obvious reasons.

Gerry Lopez - *Pipeline Virtuoso*

Gerry Lopez has stood the test of time. Twenty-five years ago, he was the best at the Pipeline. He still is one of the best. Gerry dances at the Pipeline. He is the Rudolf Nureyev of surfing, who makes riding a wave at the Pipeline seem like a ballet. What is most amazing is that Gerry, along with the young guns, is blazing new trails on killer deep water waves at Jaws on Maui. The "tow in" surfing breakthrough challenges the courage of young and conditioned athletes. Gerry Lopez is still in there.

"Gerry Lopez, still the man."

Doji Isaka

It is difficult being the first. Hiromi "Doji" Isaka was the first Japanese surfer to break into the North Shore scene. He came from a land with small surf but with people of strong will. Can you imagine coming to Hawai'i and representing your country in the first Smirnoff contest in large surf when the waves in your homeland rarely exceeded 5 feet? I could sense that Doji was not that thrilled about paddling out into the lineup in the contest, but he did it. Doji took his surfing home to Japan and made a business of it. Doji is one of Japan's surfing pioneers in the waves of Hawai'i.

Peter Cole — *a Pure Surfer*

You could walk up to Peter Cole and say, "Hey, Peter, great to see you. I just returned from orbit on the space shuttle and an asteroid is going to hit the earth tomorrow and cause the end of the world." Peter's response would be, "Shucks, we better go surfing today." Peter is a pure surfer, always has been. He still rides big waves on his BIG board.

I'd better tell you this story before Peter writes his surfing book.

I took math from Mr. Cole in high school. At the time I had a three-night-a-week job parking cars at the Tapa Room in Waikiki. I came home from work at 1 a.m. One day I fell asleep in Peter Cole's math class and he was kind enough to let me sleep through two entire subsequent classes. I awoke in a haze and to the roar of laughter from my classmates. Peter Cole is still laughing. The fact that I fell asleep in his class may not have been a reflection on his stimulating teaching skills.

The Trendsetters

Pro surfing was a tough business for the original surfers. They traveled around the world, seeking victory in contests with award money that would not even cover their travel expenses. The 1970 Smirnoff awarded only $4,600 in prize money. If you weren't in the finals, you won nothing. Shall I list the "trendsetters" who were the first pros? Nah, better not—long list, and I will probably leave someone out. In retrospect, being the first has its recompense but oftentimes is arduous. All the pro surfers reaping the rewards of modern pro competition owe a debt of gratitude to the pros of the early seventies. They made it happen.

Two contemporary trendsetters are Sunny Garcia and Kelly Slater. I am very fond of Sunny. He and my son, Heath, grew up surfing together. Though I really don't know him, Kelly Slater is an ace, too. I read about him often. He is a great role model.

Sunny Garcia performs his magic. Though the pros seem to fly on the face of waves with effortless ease, they work hard—real hard—to make it all happen.

Kaipo Guerrero launches at Pinballs, inside Waimea.
Kaipo's dad, Ants Guerrero and I were surfing and
paddling buddies in the sixties.

Feathering Trends of Future Waves

The world of the future is ours to make.

In many ways, we can do more to control our destiny. To do so, our vision must see beyond the present. We must search out truth to find the answers to the difficult questions that challenge us. I do believe there are common sense solutions to the problems that confront surfers, our communities, our nation and the world. As said before, I want to help plant the seeds of trees whose shade I will never be comforted by.

Localism?

Some North Shore regulars considered the surfers who flocked to Hawai'i every winter "guests," oftentimes uninvited. The invasion of foreign wave riders, an army of photographers and off-shore commercial interests started in the sixties and has escalated. The situation sometimes creates strife, with locals feeling Hawai'i waves are being exploited and monopolized by outsiders. Is that the price that Hawai'i surfers have to pay for living at the epicenter of world surfing? Do the surfers who call Hawai'i home have a franchise on Hawai'i waves? Is that franchise further extended to select ethnic groups, or those who speak pidgin English or take on the appearance of being local? Is it fair? If it's a problem that manifests itself in militant localism, what can be done about it? Is the world fracturing with alleged "group" rights preempting individual rights—for instance, "I'm local, beat it."? Is localism a problem that is plaguing the sport as surfing explodes in popularity? These are questions that we need to deal with.

Too Crowded

I promised myself in writing this book about my years of surfing that I would not go off on tangents. But...I feel so strongly about overpopulation that I am compelled to bring it up. Most of the world's environmental problems are byproducts of a much more serious and all-encompassing crisis, overpopulation. Our planet can no longer adequately support all the people and, most importantly, crowding is a hindrance to the quality of life. I feel crowds have a tremendous impact on an individual's temperament. When boarding a plane that is not packed, the passengers are much more laid back than the aggressive crowd boarding a full airline flight.

My belief is that crowding promotes aggression—check out a city as compared to the country. A throng at a surf site is the best evidence of how excessive crowding promotes aggression. In honestly assessing my surfing life, I can say that one of the reasons I don't surf as much as I would like to is that it is too darn crowded. In writing about the Hawai'i I grew up in 30 short years ago, I recall that we sometimes had to seek out friends to surf with in order not to be alone. Look at it now. Most politicians and alleged leaders are not addressing the issue of overpopulation. Every problem has a solution. We must

Crowding has created a new hazard in surfing. Flying bodies and loose surfboards in big surf means trouble.

stabilize world growth. Here are a few of my ideas:

- Our tax system must encourage smaller families.
- Industrialized nations should provide assistance to third world countries to help control population.
- Foreign aid by world leaders like the United States, Japan and European nations must be linked to population responsibility.
- Welfare recipients must not get paid to sit at home and have more children.
- Within the guidelines of each individual's religious beliefs, birth control must be encouraged.

Sharks

Throughout my intense surfing career in the sixties, I rarely ever saw a shark. Ironically, in the summer of 1983 I was alone, paddling a surfboard from Wailau Valley to Kalaupapa, on the north shore of Moloka'i. A shark's fin surfaced like a submarine con tower several feet to the side of my board. My heart went into overdrive as I veered toward shore. The rather large shark pursued me. I looked back and the shark straggled along behind, as I frantically stroked for the rocky coastline. The shark was not aggressive, maybe sensing that my 11-foot board was more than it could chew. The experience made me realize, once again, how vulnerable surfers are in the ocean.

Hawai'i, in the early nineties, experienced a severe shark problem. There was a tragic shark attack way back in 1959. In the years since then, sharks were not a dilemma, until 1992, when predator tiger sharks started cruising Hawai'i's coastlines. The attacks increased, resulting in loss of limbs and lives. Experts say the shark problem may have been environmentally related to diminishing food resources. Changes in the ocean environment affect the safety and welfare of surfers.

Seemingly unrelated environmental crises do oftentimes directly affect surfing. Do you think about sharks when surfing? Does surfing at night seem like a bad idea? I think about sharks now, especially when night surfing. I don't want to be a shark's dinner.

Surf Sites, Ocean Parks

The principle of "supply and demand" applies to surfing, also. We have an overwhelming demand on surfing sites—too many surfers and not enough waves. Controlling demand through stabilizing world growth could eventually trickle down to reducing demand on surf sites. Don't hold your breath waiting. The other and more immediate solution is to increase supply of surf sites.

All of us who surf and enjoy the sporting lifestyle of Hawai'i must be strong advocates of the sports industry and work to have civic leadership recognize Hawai'i as a water sports mecca. Surf sites are parks. On the North Shore there are several tennis courts at Sunset Beach School. The taxpayers paid big money to build them. There is a splendid bike and jogging path from Waimea to Paumalu. These assets are beneficial to the people of the North Shore and all of Hawai'i. Unfortunately, one of Hawai'i's most famous sports venues, Paumalu (Sunset Beach), has had little or no public infrastructure. Amenities such as parking, a bathhouse designed to accommodate competition staging and improved traffic management should be put in at Paumalu. Makaha is also sadly lacking in infrastructure and amenities for surfing and water sports.

Millions are spent on land parks and fishing and sailing harbors. Little is spent on surfing sites, yet there are probably more people using Hawai'i's shorelines for surfing than any other sport. This lack of government support for surfing is evident in many surfing locations around the world. Let's do something about it.

New surf sites could be designed and created on coastlines where there is a swell but poor ocean bottom contour. We have the technology to build surf spots. There is justification to do so. This is, incidentally, another reason why surfers should be concerned about politics.

140

I enjoyed riding the first waves from the world's first artifcial wave machine in the Arizona desert, 1969.

Technology

I lament that some extremists condemn technology and even decry nations that are on the cutting edge of technological advancement. When you think about it rationally, technology and the human's ability to improve upon and compliment nature is the source of much of our adventure. I am thrilled that I don't have to surf on a 100-pound wood surfboard. The foam board has dramatically advanced surfing. Interestingly, not much has changed since the invention of foam boards, except design concepts, till now. Technology can open more doors. The jet ski is now an intricate part of the "tow in" surfing phenomenon. Jet ski technology is towing surfers into a new realm of wave riding. We can develop hybrid sports that are surfing in origin. Let's keep an open mind and our horizons broad in order to take advantage of the ultimate wave riding medium, which is the ingenuity and imagination of the human mind. If you can dream, it may be fun to try and make it happen.

I hope you have dreams, too.

Tow Ins

The new sport of "tow ins," which is jet skis towing surfers into insanely large deep-water waves, is a revolution in big wave surfing. It is profound. The level of performance in smaller surf has evolved dramatically in the last generation. Big wave surfing has not, till now. I am not sure that even many big wave riders understand some of the dynamics involved in stroking into a very large wave. In simple terms, a surfer paddling a board gets "sucked" up to the top of a big wave while paddling for the takeoff. The bigger the wave, the faster the water is moving up the face of the wave. The reason is complicated. Every big wave photo you have seen shows the surfers hanging at the top of the wave on the takeoff. There is a point in big wave riding where the "suck up" makes it impossible to get down the wall by paddling. Surfers often free fall down the face of the large waves. The resulting wipeouts are grim. Big wave specialists dating back to ancient times have ridden long boards to get as much paddling speed as possible in order to over come the swiftness of the water racing up the face of the wave. The dynamics of big wave riding have not changed, until now. "Tow ins" have allowed surfers to overcome the problem of trying to paddle into a big wave. It has resulted in "tow in" surfers riding shorter, heavier boards. They are surfing 7-foot, weighty boards with stirrups. These boards have less wet surfaces for more speed, are heavier in order not to skip out, and stirrups keep the rider strapped on the board. This is a dramatic departure from the traditional big wave boards. The jet ski operator towing the surfer has to be intensely skillful. "Tow in" is a profound change in big wave riding that I marvel at. What "tow in" pioneers Laird Hamilton, David Kalama, Gerry Lopez and others are doing is untamed sport. They are on the edge of a new frontier of wave riding. The photos of these thrill seekers in the face of waves over 30 feet are scarce to be believed. No one has been punished by a major wipeout...yet. I hope whoever it is, survives.

Many thought we were nuts in the sixties, when we were stroking into big Makaha and Waimea waves. The intrepid surfers getting towed into the huge deep-water breaks like Jaws are really crazed. They are on the cusp of a new realm of surfing and I am in awe of tow-in surfers' courage and talent.

A classic cover shot has Laird Hamilton in the trough of a 35(?) foot wave. Jaws Maui™ is a book to behold.

Going Airborne

Surfers are starting to soar. I notice surfers are launching into more maneuvers in the air. There is also the new sport of sky surfing. The sky surfers need better air foils to fly on, and wave riders need better aqua-air foils to ride on. Surfboard design must be innovative and imaginative. Surfers could put spring-loaded wings in the rails of boards. Step on a trigger when in the air on a windy day and 3-foot-long wings would pop out of the rails. That would give the surfer a 6-foot wing, or close to an 8-foot wing span, if you include the width of the board. Ever see a seagull hang glide on the updraft of a wave? Wings on surfboards could make surfing on real windy days interesting. A young test pilot, Rush Randall, is quickly becoming "Jonathan Livingston surfer"—he is soaring. Who can stay up the longest? We'll start clocking air time.

Jet Assisted Takeoff

At an air show I recently attended, a prop aircraft took off. Less than a hundred feet off the ground, rocket jets strapped on the side of the plane kicked in and the lumbering craft pointed up and climbed to over a thousand feet in less than a minute. They call it a JATO takeoff. We have the technology to create new experiences in surfing. Why not build into the tail blocks of surfboards tiny self-contained jet bottles? Imagine what could be done with a high-powered 3- to 5-second blast from the tail of a board in a critical position on an impossible wave. Put on the stirrups and let's blast off.

Helmets — *for the hard-core wave warriors*

Helmets are a good idea, especially at breaks like the Pipeline. The evolution of better helmets has made them functional. The year the Duke Team went to the Huntington Beach contest in the sixties, we were required to wear helmets. They were antiquated, and surfing with them on seemed like having an anchor on your head. Those helmets would protect your head while you drowned.

New state-of-the-art helmets are not cumbersome. They are functional. Let's improve on them. A big wave helmet could be designed that has a small air cylinder attached. A high-tech mouthpiece could supply those few breaths of air necessary to save a surfer from drowning in giant waves. Helmets can also be very functional sun blocks. Ask any senior surfer about sun-related problems. Here is an illuminating idea. How about a helmet with two high-powered lights attached to the side for night surfing? I jog the Koʻolau Mountain trails on full moon nights (it is where I encounter the spirits of my soul). On the night runs, I tape two powerful flashlights to a mountain bike helmet. The light is always pointed where my eyes are looking— works great. The same could be done for night surfing.

Hawaiian Outrigger Canoes

The genius of the Hawaiian outrigger canoe is that it is an ocean vehicle that has been in existence for over 1,000 years. The design is simple, yet profound. An outrigger canoe can traverse great distances of open ocean and then maneuver to shore over a shallow reef. The Hawaiian outrigger canoe can ride a wave, be propelled by a sail and, of course, by paddle power. Can you think of any other ocean-going boat that has that versatility?

Racing a traditional outrigger canoe across a channel in the Hawaiian Islands is atavistic.

144

In 1968 the Outrigger Canoe Club team barely survived huge swells—the race really was an epic man against the sea adventure. We made it.

Canoe Surfing

My buddy Pat Bowlen and I were on the beach at Makaha for Buffalo's big board contest's first canoe surfing event. Pat and I have been riding waves in canoes for years. Canoe surfing, when you really get into it, is like surfing, except you are in a 24-foot canoe that weighs several hundred pounds. The similarity is "trimming." On takeoff the weight should shift back. Holding a canoe in a slide is difficult. The crew, in this case, Pat, has to do all the trimming and balancing of the boat. After doing it for 20 years on waves from 1 foot to close to 15 feet, Pat and I don't have to say much to each other when riding a wave. It all comes naturally. Pat is smart enough to understand that the canoe steersman is the handsome and smart person who is "da captain" and all he has to do is maintain trim and get his butt kicked when we wipe out.

Buffalo's big board contest has helped revive interest in canoe surfing competition. In March of '97 my son, Heath, called and asked me to come out to the contest and steer his "Local 808" crew. When I got to the beach, I found myself surrounded by a group of top-shape young wave warriors. We had never been in a canoe together. The crew were experienced watermen. We made the finals in rough 8-foot surf. We wiped out often. That is part of the challenge—to see how long you can hang on. Pure fun, but wipeouts are dangerous. The great thing about canoe surfing is that no one gets in your way. Surfers are smart enough not to risk getting run over by a canoe.

Pat and I had a few good waves at Buffalo's first canoe surfing competition. Riding Makaha in a canoe is a trip...excuse the sixties twaddle.

145

Photographers, Artists and Authors

Surfing is the most aesthetic sport in the world, at least I think so. Surf photographers are the original artists of surfing. Dr. Don James, Leroy Grannis, Warren Bolster, Don King, Aaron Chang and Jeff Divine are a few of the renowned and innovative photographers of the formative years. In the publishing world, a few surfing magazines are also works of art.

Speaking of art, I have always believed that art helps define culture. In recent years surfing has spawned artists of diverse disciplines.

In the early eighties, I hired a talented surfing artist, Ken Auster, to produce art for a Triple Crown poster. He also made limited edition prints. The poster depicts a Hawaiian hula dancer in a refrain pose as surfers skim across the front of her skirt. Ken produced a surfing classic. Surfing has developed art and culture.

I recently read a novel *The Dogs of Winter,* by Kem Nunn. Another well-written and researched novel is *Caught Inside*, by surfer Daniel Duane. Surfers are becoming provocative authors, writing with substance and style. As a result, I feel our sport is developing an intellect beyond "how's the surf?"

I love the feeling of this poster. Artist Ken Auster created a classic.

146

Biarritz

The surfing culture has a legacy from ancient Hawai'i. The Biarritz Surf Festival, held every summer, captures the spirit of surfing. It is classic. Ricky Grigg and I wrote an editorial about Biarritz upon returning home to Hawai'i after the 1993 festival.

This is my version of the editorial before Ricky edited it to include his perspective and it was published.

Biarritz Surf Festival
1993

A traditional Basque band was playing music and hundreds of cheering people greeted surfing legends as they arrived in Biarritz, France. Our Hawaiian group were guests of the Biarritz Surf Festival. The week long event was hosted by the city of Biarritz and produced by the devoted Robert Rabagny, his wife, Patricia and staff. In addition to cultural events such as an art show, music, films and commerce, the festival featured a long board surfing championship with a $30,000 purse. The Festival garnered French national television, radio and print media coverage. Thousands flocked to the seashore every day to share in the festivities, meet the surfing legends and watch the competition.

As fate would have it, Reynolds Wright, a jovial surfer from Waianae was featured on the logo for the festival. Little did the French know that they had selected a Hawaiian full of merriment, fun and laughter to be the poster boy of the Biarritz Surf Festival. Reynolds's picture was plastered on posters, signs and billboards all over the Basque country. He was featured on T-shirts, key chains, bags and even the label of a commemorative bottle of wine. Reynolds is probably one of the most recognized sports faces in Biarritz but relatively unknown in his native Hawaii. Reynolds and his brother in goodwill, Boogie Kalama, responded to the recognition and hospitality with good cheer and sowed the seeds of aloha where ever we went. The Hawai'i Visitors Bureau could not have sent better ambassadors for Hawaii.

The surfing competition began with an Hawaiian ceremony. Brian Keaulana led a procession of surfers with boards under their arms to the sea. The Hawaiian surfers, clad in malu marched to the shoreline calling out a Hawaiian chant. At the edge of the Atlantic, the surfers, surrounded by their National flags carried bottles of sea water taken from their home surf. A circle was formed around a cistern into which each surfer poured their sea water. First France, then Hawaii, Australia, New Zealand, Brazil, California, East Coast, Tahiti, Spain, South Africa, Japan and the Canary Islands. The mixing of the sea water joined all in the spirit of goodwill.

The throng of surfers, including Biarritz surfing legend Joel DeRosnay, entered the sea and paddled out beyond the shore break. We formed a large circle, holding hands in unity. In the middle of the circle Brain Keaulana offered a "hookupu", a gift, to acknowledge the aloha of all present. The Biarritz Surf festival quickly evolved into a cultural milestone for the sport of surfing. The French recognize Hawai'i as the genesis of surfing. It made us, the children of the waves of Hawai'i, proud. The long board competition was won by Joel Tudor of Florida, our Rusty Keaulana was a close second, but in actuality everyone won the greater victory of sharing the aloha of the festival.

Aloha was carried to France by the surfers from Hawaii but somehow the French lifted our spirits to greater heights. As we stood in the spotlight on the faraway shores of France, many of us wondered if Hawaii may be taking for granted our surfing heritage. The names of all Hawaii's wave riding legends are revered as surfing nobility in France. It would have brought tears of joy to our beloved Duke Kahanamoku's eyes to see Hawaii's sons and daughters of the surf standing so proudly on the beach of a far away land. Brian's wife, Nobleen Keaulana, expressed our feelings so well, "The French are so proud of Hawaii's surfing heritage."

Long Board Surfing

Thank God, something I do in surfing is coming back into popularity. I never really made the transition to short boards. I want to sit outside and catch the waves before all the wave warriors on short boards. Long board surfing is back. Rusty Keaulana, Bonga Perkins and Joel Tudor are long board wizards. Here is a question to ponder. Which discipline is more difficult—long boarding or short board performing? I watch Rusty Keaulana on a long board then watch Sunny Garcia on a short board, and wonder.

I theorize that there is more happening with the reemergence of long board surfing than the obvious. Surfing exploded in the sixties and baby boomers took up the sport by the legions. Those surfers are now riding long boards. I knew it—my baby boomer friends who ventured off into short board Lala land are back to long boards. Long board surfers no longer have to prove anything. They want to catch waves, carve long, flowing turns and enjoy themselves. As more surfers mature into...let's see...middle age, they will put away the short boards and join us. Long boards rule. P.S. I am not getting old, just my body is.

Family

I feel the family is the foundation of a healthy society.

I am a second generation surfer and paddler.

In 1970 I was blessed with the birth of a son, Heath. He first rode a surfboard when he was 9 months old. I took him out on an old board of mine affectionately called the "Blue Max." As we rode a wave, he laughed and giggled, as babies will. He did not show any fear at 9 months. It has been all fun since. My daughters, Kaui and Meaghan, have made the ocean part of their lives. Suzy, my tandem partner, is the backbone of our family.

Most of us learn patience and how to raise children after they have already grown up. It is an empirical process. I learned that children often don't learn what you tell them, they learn what they experience with you. You can tell them something is bad but if you do it yourself you create a contradiction.

Remember the adage about old people who in their twilight years never regret having not spent more time at the office. I don't think anyone regrets spending time with their children.

Surfing can be a wonderful lifelong sport. Teach your kids well. Take them surfing. Spend time with them. They grow up so fast...too fast.

149

Everyone has a good time when we surf together. Years from now, my family—Kaui, Meaghan, wife Suzy and son Heath—will remember this day we caught the same wave together.

The Wealth of Hawai'i

Wealth can be measured in many ways.

I consider myself blessed and a wealthy person.

I have a vigorous and dynamic family, and enjoy good health.

Men and women of diverse backgrounds enrich my life.

I have lived in and loved Hawai'i all my life.

From the crest of Mauna Kea the cold of the snow goddess Poliahu has chilled my soul.

My heart has pounded the rhythm of a chanting drum while running across the blistering lava fields of Kona.

Upon the peak of Haleakala I have felt the golden rays of the dawn's sun caress these Islands.

In the dark loneliness of Papalaua valley on Moloka'i I have heard the wind whisper of ancient Hawai'i.

My back has ached from countless strokes while racing a koa canoe across the Kaiwi channel.

In the shadow of Konahuanui I have felt the warrior's ghosts.

I have danced with the waves in the soft light of a full moon night.

I have glided across the face of azure walls of water while surfing the mystical waves of these islands of Hawai'i.

I am a child of the waves.

I am a surfer.

All of this is my wealth.

Aloha...

Thank you to these contributors:

The following are photographers of great renown
in the surf world.
Kirk Aeder, Warren Bolster, Aaron Chang,
Ron Church, Peter French, Leroy Grannis,
Don James Estate, Tom Keck and Phil Wilson

And special mahalo to:

Dave Parmenter, The Honolulu Advertiser,
The Outrigger Duke Kahanamoku Foundation,
personal photos of Fred Hemmings Sr.,
Surfer Magazine, Honolulu Magazine
and Tim McCullough.